TYNESIDE: WHERE'S THE BUZZ

Your def
to England's N

Everybody who comes to Tyneside feels *the buzz*:

From Saturday night revellers soaking up the electric atmosphere of Newcastle's pub and club scene, to diners at the region's many top restaurants...

From Theatre Royal audiences milling in the foyer for opera, ballet or the Royal Shakespeare Company, to families watching a big-name act in one of the country's top working men's clubs...

From the pubs and restaurants on the Quayside under Tyneside's famous bridges to great sporting events like the Great North Run...

There's a real *buzz* on Tyneside. And this book will show you where to find it.

Whether you're looking for the liveliest pub, or the most traditional; an exclusive, expensive restaurant or a cheap "little gem" with good food, we'll help you find it. Whether you're into sport, history or the arts, we'll help you find somewhere with *a buzz*...

Cover picture: Geordie Princess

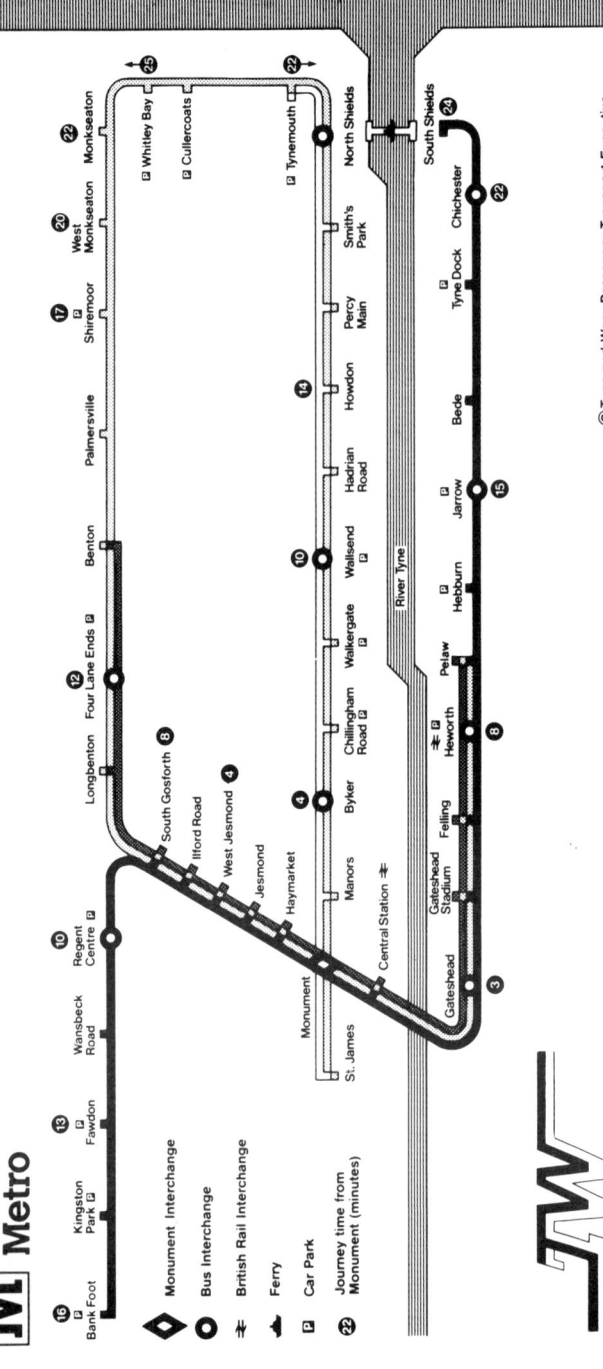

TYNESIDE
WHERE'S THE BUZZ

EDITED BY
Richard Falkner

BLOODAXE BOOKS

Copyright © Bloodaxe Books (Projects) Ltd 1989

ISBN: 1 85557 000 9

First published 1989 by
Bloodaxe Books (Projects) Ltd,
P.O. Box 1SN,
Newcastle upon Tyne NE99 1SN.

Editorial assistant: Kate Donovan.
Cover photographs: Moira Conway.
City photographs: City of Newcastle upon Tyne City Engineer's Dept (pages 7, 9, 11, 12, 100).
Other photographs: Sirkka-Liisa Konttinen (pages 16, 44, 125), Moira Conway, Richard Falkner and organisations featured.
Paste-up: Thanks to Jan.

LEGAL NOTICE
All rights reserved. No part of this book may be reproduced, stored in a retrieval system, or transmitted in any form, or by any means, electronic, mechanical, photocopying, recording or otherwise, without prior written permission from the publisher.

Typesetting by E.F. Peterson & Son, South Shields.

Printed in Great Britain by
Billings & Sons Limited, Worcester.

EDITOR'S NOTE

We have tried to ensure that the information in this book is as accurate and up-to-date as possible. We have used over a dozen researchers, and pubs, clubs, restaurants, museums, galleries and local councils have been circularised to try to make sure that this guide is as comprehensive as we can make it. However, it is almost inevitable that some mistakes will have crept into this work. In addition, during the shelf-life of a work of this kind, new establishments will open, staff will leave, restaurants will change hands or even close, and information will become out of date.

I would therefore like to apologise in advance for any omissions, errors or mistakes in this edition. If anybody has any comments about the book or its contents or thinks it needs correcting or updating in any way, we would be glad to hear from them. We will endeavour to check out any suggestions for the next edition!

I would like to thank all those researchers and contributors who have helped produce this book on time, and also all those who have responded to our questionnaires. In particular, I would like to thank Kate Donovan, for producing the maps and collating the material so ably, Linda Healy for assisting with the typesetting, Diane Jamieson for her enthusiastic work, and Moira Conway for taking the cover pictures and many of the photographs inside the book.

RICHARD FALKNER

HOW TO USE THIS BOOK

Geordieland has got to be one of the best places in the world!

For People, Places, Music, Sport, Theatre, Pubs, Restaurants, Cinemas, Art...Everything!

We want you to know just a little more of what's on offer in the real Tyneside. Not just the gourmet restaurants and best real ale pubs (which you get in some guides), but...

● The pubs where you get singsongs round the piano, an alternative cabaret or exciting up-and-coming rock bands.

● Restaurants where you can have a great night out for a fiver, the best home-made pasta or top vegetarian cooking.

● The small theatres, galleries, museums and music venues (classical, jazz, rock and folk) where you can see what the region's writers, actors, artists, photographers and film/video makers and musicians are doing – and probably meet them in the bar.

We'll tell you...

● Where the students go, where the bikers go and where the yuppies go.

● The smart places and the off-the-beaten track places.

● The place to go hang gliding, skiing in summer, bowling, golfing, riding, five-a-siding, windsurfing and ponytrekking – we'll even tell you where to take flying lessons!

And that's just for starters...

PUBS

RESTAURANTS

CLUBS

PLACES TO SE

THE ARTS

SPORT

A Message to Southerners

The North may begin at Watford, but *the buzz* starts *here!*

There's no doubt about it: Tyneside is a beautiful place, a-buzz with a unique culture which always surprises first-time visitors and constantly delights the people who live here! But, like anywhere else, whether you are planning to stay for a few days or for a lifetime, it pays to get to know it.

If you come from the south, probably the first thing you'll have to get out of your mind is coal – 'Coals to Newcastle'. Tyneside used to be full of coal and heavy industry, but not any more. If you want to see all that, you'll have to look for it in museums – like the superb Beamish Museum or the F-Pit Museum, just down the

● **The top sporting event in June is the Great North Run. 25,000 athletes swarm along the roads from Newcastle to South Shields in Europe's biggest half-marathon.**

road at Washington. You'll find that Newcastle is an unexpectedly beautiful, traditional city; you'll find Europe's first out-of-town shopping mall at the incredible Gateshead MetroCentre; and you'll find a rapid transport system which makes London's underground look like something out of the Dark Ages, Tyneside's Metro.

But don't forget the pits and heavy industry entirely: remember the high personal price Tynesiders have recently paid (and many are still paying) in jobs, cash and real family hardship when so many of the outdated coalmines and steelworks and shipyards were swept away. Don't patronise us. Remember that it was pioneering Tynesiders like George Stephenson, Charles Parsons, Joseph Swan and Lord Armstrong who virtually invented the Industrial Revolution.

Don't be misled by your cloth-cap preconceptions: Geordies go back a long way before Victorian times. Northumbria was already way up-market culturally and intellectually when you southerners were still more interested in hunting wild boars than in learning to read.

In Roman times, Tyneside, at one end of the still impressive Hadrian's Wall, marked the northernmost boundary of civilisation. A few centuries later, in the Middle Ages, it was already a world capital of culture. It was in Jarrow that the Venerable Bede wrote his famous history in 731. It was at Durham that the itinerant Lindisfarne monks, who for over a hundred years had carried the miraculously undecayed body of one of Britain's greatest saints, St Cuthbert, finally decided to lay his body to rest, laying the foundations of one of Christendom's most impressive cathedrals.

Today, the region still makes an impressive mark on the national culture, from pop music to great literature: Geordies Hank Marvin and Bruce Welch helped make British pop music before the Beatles had been heard of. Alan Price, Sting, The Animals, Mark Knopfler and Lindisfarne are major names in popular music – and all are Geordies.

● Newcastle's Grey Street, built by John Dobson in the 1830s.

> My days of serious enjoyment on Tyneside were in the 1950s, when I was a student at King's. Those good times were mostly in and around pubs like the Royal Oak and the Dun Cow, behind the University, the Empire and Palace Theatres, the Oxford Galleries and the Old Assembly Rooms, and an assortment of snooker halls, including the Dial in Northumberland Street. Most of these temples of pleasure seem to have disappeared or changed their names, in the name of somebody's progress, though he didn't leave a name. Smart feller. Nowadays I head straight for the Quayside and Live Theatre, which welcomes writers like Tom Hadaway, Michael Chaplin, Phil Woods and Leonard Barras. It's a good place to see upfront plays and there's a bar to match. The beer's fine and all round it's a perfect spot to solve the problems of the Universe. If there are *very* important problems to solve we take a turn around the block and pause at the Crown Posada. I've also been promised a game of snooker in Byker at the Supasnooker Centre, which I'm told is good value.
> ● ALAN PLATER, PLAYWRIGHT

Tyneside is currently a major centre for writers. It is the home of Britain's most successful novelist, Catherine Cookson (on South Tyneside there is a trail where you can follow in the footsteps of her fictional heroes and heroines), and television's Alan Plater (*A Very British Coup*...), Ian La Frenais (*Auf Wiedersehen, Pet, The Likely Lads*...), Rowan Atkinson, Miriam Stoppard and Kate Adie all hail from the region. Basil Bunting, one of the greatest poets this century, was born on the banks of the Tyne and lived in the area in his later years, until his death in 1985. The great 18th century artist Thomas Bewick was a Northumbrian. On the sport side, the North East is home to great athletes such as Steve Cram and Brendan Foster, and footballers Bobby and Jackie Charlton. Other famous Geordies include Stan Laurel, Cardinal Basil Hume and opera singer Thomas Allen.

The regional television station, Tyne Tees Television, is based on Tyneside, and the BBC have a major television and radio centre here. There are also three locally-based radio stations, the commercial station, Metro Radio, BBC Radio Newcastle, and the new station, Great North Radio.

Shoppers travel hundreds of miles to visit our huge indoor shopping centres, the Gateshead MetroCentre and Eldon Square in Newcastle. (They even come by ferry from Norway!) Coachloads of young adults come from far and wide to enjoy the incredible nightlife, and arts lovers, too, come from Yorkshire, Scotland and the other side of the country, to visit our theatres.

Some southerners say we're too far away from the rest of the country, but we say we're in just the right place: beautiful sandy beaches on one side, and rolling dales on the other. To the north is one of Britain's wildest and least-explored counties, Northumberland, with its wonderful beaches, fantastic castles and miles upon miles of deserted hills. To the south, the land of the Prince Bishops and one of the world's finest architectural achievements, Durham Cathedral.

Being 'so far away' has plenty of advantages – for one we are used to arranging our own entertainment! While many councils in the so-called Home Counties are reluctant to fund the arts 'because it's all just up the road in London', Tyneside offers an arts programme of drama, music, ballet, opera and film which is often envied by those who live in London – because here there isn't the hassle or the expense!

There are several good cinemas, including the ten-screen Cannon cinema in the Gateshead MetroCentre which runs the latest top films, the new Warner Brothers ten-screen cinema at Manors, Newcastle's four-screen Odeon, and the Tyneside Cinema, in Pilgrim Street, Newcastle, which shows a range of trendy, alternative, artistic and foreign films. And sports venues range from the internationally-renowned Gateshead Stadium to Newcastle Racecourse at Gosforth and St James's Park, home of the Magpies, Newcastle United.

IS THIS HOW Northerners used to see Southerners? It's *The Wild Man of the Woods*, an engraving by Thomas Bewick, Northumbria's greatest artist who worked on the smallest scale. You can watch original prints being made from his own blocks at the Bewick Birthplace Museum at Cherryburn.

WHERE'S THE BUZZ

But there's plenty of tradition too: like the Hoppings, Europe's biggest funfair made up by several travelling fairs all coming together on the Town Moor for one week in June. Like the working men's clubs. Like the Lindisfarne Christmas concerts held every year at the City Hall which have become as much an institution as carol services are in other parts of the country.

There is a great deal of enthusiasm in Tyneside and much natural exuberance. But if one thing distinguishes Tyneside from other places it is its total lack of pretension. This is what Geordie humour and much of the culture is all about. When the Royal Shakespeare Company first started coming to Newcastle, the actors loved it for one reason above all others: they got an honest response from the public. They didn't laugh at the intellectual in-jokes or nod knowingly at the artistic nuances, they took the work at face value, and loved it. And came in their droves. And they do the same with ballet, opera, classical music and rock concerts. It's not that Geordies don't know the intellectual niceties (be warned, they're pretty sharp!), it's just that they can't stand snobs, especially intellectual snobs.

From high cuisine to fish 'n' chips, you'll get as fine a day or night out on Tyneside as you will anywhere. The difference is that on Tyneside the quality you get for the price is frequently superb.

But one word of warning. Whatever you decide to do on Tyneside, don't do it shyly. They'll never let you get away with it...

Tyneside's Best Free Shows

One of Tyneside's best free shows is the Quayside market on a Sunday morning. Allowed by an ancient Act of Parliament, the market is the place to go for a huge variety of things from ironmongery to magic tricks, with the inevitable kitchen gadgets, crockery and linen thrown in. Watch the false auctions, listen to the patter of the sellers, but be careful you know exactly what you're buying before you part with any cash!

If you enjoy cycling, or fancy a longer walk, take to the south side of the river, across the Swing Bridge, and walk up river along the newly-landscaped embankment.

Other good free shows include political activists and street musicians at Grey's Monument, Newcastle (particularly on a Saturday), the visitor's gallery in the magistrates court in Market Street (11am weekdays – get there early!), the boats coming in and out of the river at Tynemouth (take the Metro to Tynemouth and turn right at the Priory – then wait!), watching the students revising in the summer (they doze in the sunshine around Leazes Lake), and watching the indoor funfair at Gateshead's Metro Centre (buses run to the MetroCentre from Grey's Monument in

● Spectacular firework displays are staged on the Tyne. This one marked the launch of the Tall Ships Race from Newcastle.

the centre of Newcastle). Paddy Freeman's Lake (above Jesmond Dene) is always worth a visit when the men are running round with their model boats. And if you think the Bigg Market on a Friday or Saturday night is lively, take the Metro home at closing time with the revellers for an unforgettable party on wheels!

For a complete guide to the free shows you missed and the ones that might be coming soon, see Tyneside's evening paper, the *Evening Chronicle*. As well as carrying advertising for most theatre, film and music events, it carries extensive What's On columns.

At the Central Library, in Princess Square, just behind Northumberland Street, you'll find copies of free listing magazines with details of the month's events. *Index* tends to be arts orientated, while *Paint It Red* is good for rock and pop music.

Metro Radio is also a good, free show. As well as weather and traffic news, the DJs belt out details of local events, especially at weekends. Make sure you listen to Alan Robson's *Night Owls* (where insomniacs who think they haven't got problems or opinions can listen to the DJ being driven demented by people who think they have).

● **The Sunday market on the Quayside is one of Newcastle's most popular free shows.**

Where Do You Start?

The scenery is free! With its imposing river bridges, fine buildings and wide open spaces (there are whole moors in the middle of Newcastle!), Tyneside is a good place to explore on foot or on a bike, particularly on a Sunday.

Take a walk up Jesmond Dene, a dramatic valley, part natural, partly artificially created by armaments supremo Lord Armstrong, who used to live in what is now the (up-market) Fisherman's Lodge restaurant. You can walk along the dene all the way from Heaton Library, through Heaton Park and Armstrong Park, to South Gosforth. Make sure you go far enough northwards to see the old mill with its quaint bridge and waterfall. On Sundays there is a craft market on Armstrong Bridge which is much frequented by students and trendies from Jesmond.

The Town Moor is another huge area just to the north of the city, a stone's throw from the city centre. In summer, cattle graze there and for one week in June virtually the whole of this vast area between Newcastle and Gosforth is taken over by The Hoppings. Claimed to be Europe's biggest travelling fair, it boasts hundreds of rides, stalls and scores of fortune-tellers, freak shows, sideshows, shooting galleries and the like. For the rest of the year it is very quiet except when it snows. Then the hills which mark the site of the old Leazes pit come alive with students skiing, sledging and sliding down on anything they can lay their hands on.

But for a real walk, you need to get out to the coast, to Tynemouth, Cullercoats or Whitley Bay, and head out along the sands.

But first get the geography right...

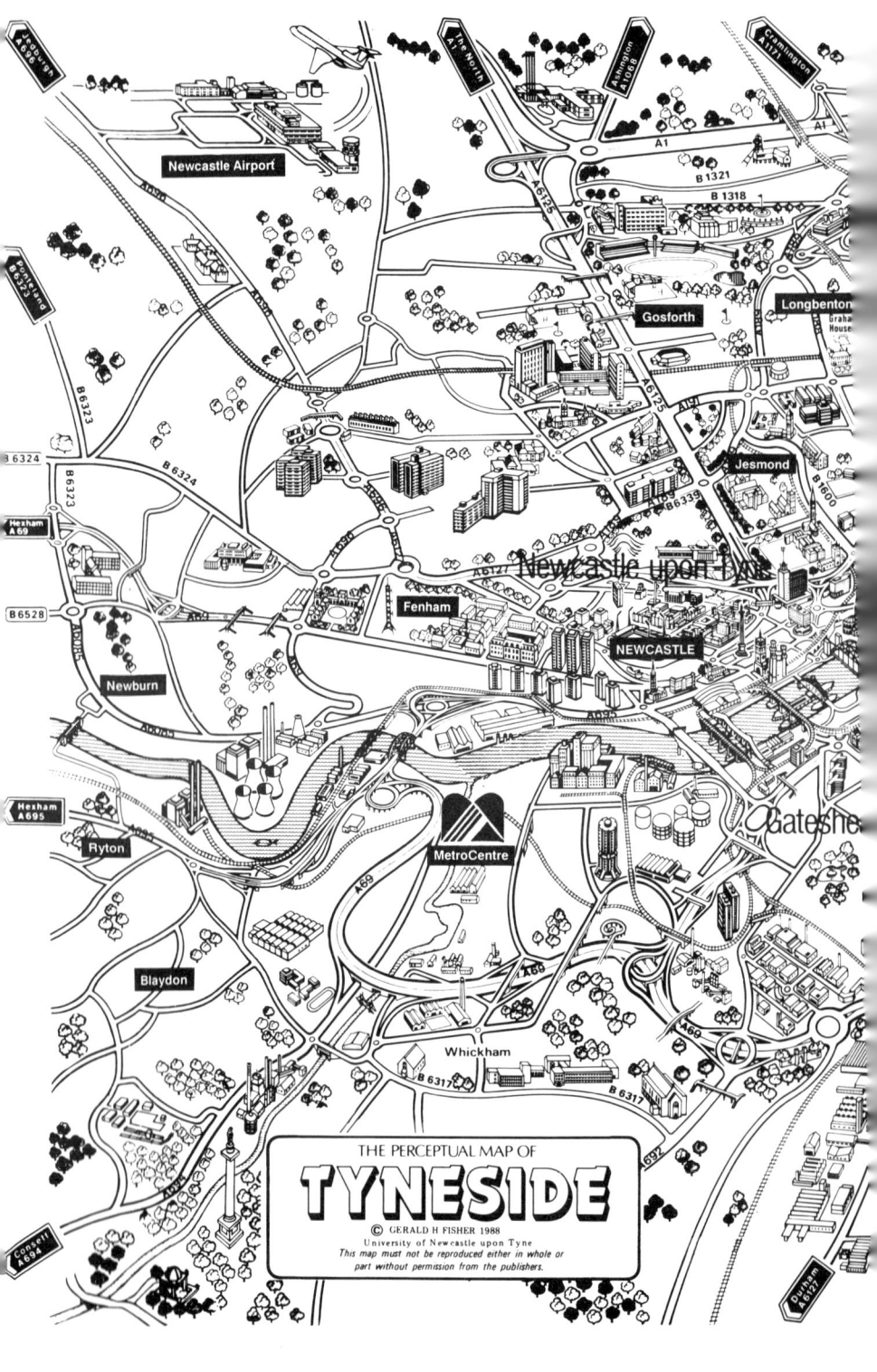

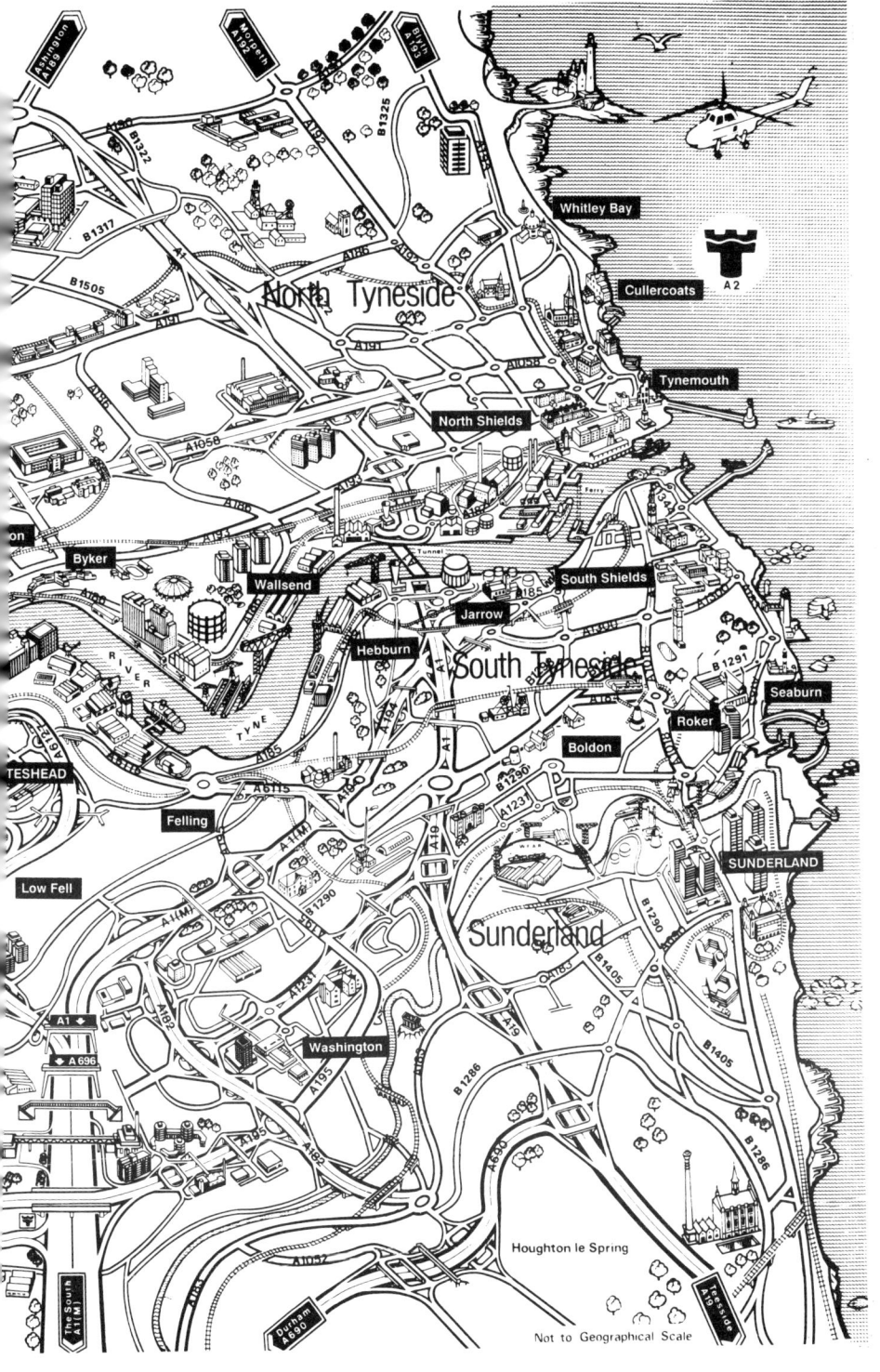

PUBS

If it hadn't been for religion, Tyneside would be stiff with pubs. As it is, there are alehouses only on *nearly* every corner. In the trendy places like Jesmond and Heaton, there are very few: most are clustered around the edges. It's all because the land was once owned by Quakers, and when the houses were built it was made a condition that no pubs should be built there.

The result is that the two areas where most newcomers to Newcastle live, and where many visitors stay, are very badly off for pubs. And the pubs which are there tend to be rather disappointing. Which may be one of the reasons you sometimes hear people who don't know the area well enough complaining that there are 'no decent pubs'.

In fact, Tyneside has many good pubs. There are pubs of every kind and description in dazzling (or at least blurring) profusion, from country pubs to wine bars, to disco bars to homely locals.

If you want an example of comfort, luxury, good beer, good food and fine views (with live music thrown in), go straight to the **Wooden Doll** at North Shields.

If you want a friendly, traditional Geordie pub, try the **Black Bull** at Blaydon. Or go to the back bar at the **New Clarendon** at

● Regulars enjoy a singalong at the New Clarendon in North Shields. Photograph by Sirkka-Liisa Konttinen.

North Shields on a Saturday night, order yourself a bottle of Newcastle Brown (you'll get it in the traditional way, with a half-pint short balloon glass to pour out and keep topping up, bit by bit) and sit amongst the regulars singing songs around the piano.

On the other hand, if you want to see Newcastle's young set at its trendiest and most exuberant, try the open air public party that is Newcastle's Bigg Market on a Friday or Saturday night. It's not for the faint-hearted or the young at heart, only for the genuinely young. But you can't beat the excitement of hundreds of youngsters crammed together in the pubs and bars (you have to queue for the doormen – you mustn't call them bouncers – to let you in as others come out).

Friday night is traditionally the night when the lads and lasses go out separately. Saturday is when they go out as couples. Don't be intimidated by the police or the gangs. Remember there are literally thousands of youngsters in town, most of them more concerned with looking good (jeans and designer-shirts and skimpy dresses whatever the weather) than with other people. Considering the numbers, the amount of trouble is astonishingly low. But if you do come across any, whatever you do, don't get involved.

Once in the pub, two tips. If you want a scotch, ask for a whisky. If you ask for scotch you'll get a pint of best Scotch beer. And if someone mentions the dog, don't look down at your shoes. Dog is Newcastle Brown Ale, also called the Broon. So whether you're driving or not, remember to keep the dog under control.

***Tyneside, Where's the Buzz* was compiled from a wide range of reports from over a dozen anonymous researchers, who regularly use the pubs, restaurants and other facilities listed as paying customers.**

REAL ALE

Ten years ago, when the Campaign for Real Ale brought out its first monthly magazine in this area, less than one pub in ten sold any form of cask-conditioned ale – that is beer which contains basic ingredients (ideally only water, malted barley, hops and yeast), is allowed to ferment in the cask, and is served without the addition of gas.

Now the choice is somewhat wider and Tyneside boasts a long and varied list of real ale outlets. There are pubs offering good food, quality entertainment, atmospheres to suit all tastes and, still, some basic boozers out of the spit-and-sawdust mould. Obviously beer quality does vary but all pubs mentioned in this section will almost always serve a pint that is well conditioned and cared for.

Unfortunately, pub opening hours are still in an experimental phase and it is worth checking afternoon opening times which may change with the time of year.

Almost directly opposite the Central Station in Newcastle is the **Forth Hotel**. Yorkshiremen inform me that this pub offers the finest Tetley Bitter in the North East. The food on offer at lunchtimes is certainly good, although the choice is somewhat limited. Jennings Bitter and Tetley Imperial complete the portfolio of ales. The place was recently renovated, but this was achieved tastefully and without destroying too much of its character.

Turn right at the station and you should find the **Bridge Hotel**, next to the High Level Bridge. This is the first of several city pubs owned by Sir John Fitzgeralds, a property and free house which maintains some fine real ale outlets. The Bridge beer garden, in summer, offers one of Newcastle's few *al fresco* drinking areas. This garden has not one blade of grass but does have superb views of the Tyne, the railway and the city walls. Beers offered are Theakstons XB and Bitter, Tetley Bitter and usually a guest ale. The atmosphere is always friendly.

Down the steps from the castle opposite the Bridge will bring you to Newcastle Quayside. Here there is the **Cooperage** which dates from the 14th century and is now a Tetley Free House with Bitter, Imperial and a selection of guest ales (most, though not all, from the Allied chain). Superb food makes this a popular

● **The Bridge Hotel is one of Newcastle's few remaining traditional city pubs.**

lunchtime resort for the city's business people. The beer is a little pricey but you do not need to be wealthy to enjoy a couple of pints and a hot beef sandwich. There is also a full range of bar meals and a restaurant as well as two excellent rooms for hire for any sort of meeting.

Also on the Quayside is the **Red House**. This is an enormous sprawling building with one bar catering for the real ale drinker. It serves a wide and constantly varying range of beers with a choice of about four or five at a time. Sandwiches and simple hot food are available at lunchtimes with more substantial fare in the restaurant or wine bar. It is also a perfect meeting-place as wide windows give a fine view of passers-by!

The nearby **Crown Posada** was Tyneside and Northumberland's Pub of the Year in 1986. Popularly known as the 'Coffin' – due to its shape, not the beer – it offers an excellent Hadrian Gladiator, from Tyneside's least famous but finest brewery, plus Taylors Landlord, Stones Best Bitter, Hartleys XB and, very often, a guest as well. The pub is Victorian and sports some marvellous stained glass windows. Food at lunchtimes is limited to sandwiches and toasties but the place is usually full of CAMRA members.

Moving towards the city centre the **Duke of Wellington** is another Tetley Free House with Bitter, Imperial and a guest. Food is very good, and the pub, known locally as 'Stokoes', is often quite busy and very handy for shops and businesses. Take a look at the old photos including one of the biggest licensee in the business!

Behind the Duke of Wellington is the **Old George**. This Bass pub has some excellent meals at lunchtimes. The atmosphere changes completely in the evenings to that of a bustling city centre pub popular with students. Admission at weekend evenings can be something of a problem after about nine. Occasional live entertainments are held upstairs but the place is probably at its best for a lunchtime meal in the downstairs restaurant area.

Further along High Bridge is the **Bacchus**, another Fitzgeralds real ale pub. McEwans 80/-, Stones Bitter, Tetley Bitter, Theakstons XB and a guest ale are regularly available. There are two bars, one free of slot machines, and although some purists suggest that the ale is a little on the cold side it is definitely worth a visit. Pleasant traditional pub food is available at lunchtimes and there is a Monday evening quiz which can be fun.

Another Bass outlet in the city is the **Three Bulls Heads**. This is a large pub which has been knocked down, rebuilt and then had a

MEET ME ON THE CORNER: Lindisfarne, Tyneside's popular folk rock group, pictured supping ale at their local. *Left to right:* Ray Laidlaw, Alan Hull, Si Cowe, Rod Clements, Ray Jackson.

shopping centre extended around it. Amazingly the pub has retained its appeal and the beer has always been reliable. Watch out for the 8 o'clock leap in volume on the jukebox. Lovers of peace and quiet should time last orders for 7.45.

The **Broken Doll** on the other side of town has Theakstons beers and another loud juke box. This is a distinctive pub which often offers live music in the evenings. The clientele are obviously predominantly young and many are committed to Newcastle's thriving local music scene. Although now threatened by a road building scheme it is hoped that the place will survive long enough for readers of this guide to enjoy the good beer served and the interesting outfits worn by the staff.

Jesmond possesses a large student colony and this is reflected in the clientele at the **Lonsdale** next to West Jesmond Metro Station. One of S&N's better outlets, the Lonsdale keeps a good pint of No.3 but can be a little busy in the evenings. Food is available at lunchtimes.

Close to Manors Metro Station in Shieldfield is the **Queens Arms**. This pub has an excellent range of lunchtime meals which can be washed down with Theakstons beers in a pleasant environment. It's popular with students in the evenings.

On City Road, going east out of Newcastle, is another Fitzgeralds house. The **Rose and Crown** serves Draught Bass, Stones Best Bitter and Theakstons XB plus occasional guests, although at time of writing the licensee was talking about modifying this range of beers. It is a pleasant two-roomed local with a good following of regulars plus the overspill from the dark and noisy Scottish and Newcastle pub over the road. The Rose and Crown is a popular haunt of employees of Tyne Tees Television, whose offices are nearby.

Closer to the river is the **Free Trade Inn**, another S&N pub worthy of mention. Here there are McEwans 80/-, Youngers No.3, Theakstons XB and Theakstons Bitter. The jukebox here offers a magnificent selection of jazz favourites including the likes of Cab Calloway and Ella Fitzgerald.

The **Tap and Spile** in Byker was the first in Camerons innovative chain of real ale pubs and in its first year was CAMRA's area pub of the year. Although still not sufficiently "rough around the edges" for everyone's tastes, it does offer a wide and constantly changing selection of beers. These are always good quality and rapid turnover prevents deterioration of the product. A pint of Franklins Bitter of the highest quality imbibed on a recent visit would have been enough alone to justify this pub's inclusion in this chapter. The beer is a little expensive but to offset this the food on offer is very reasonable and the surroundings warm and comfortable.

For those who prefer fewer creature comforts and more basic pleasures there is always the **Cumberland Arms** set on a hill beside Byker Bridge overlooking the Ouseburn valley. The Cumberland has survived the ravages of time. A word of warning: this pub is not for the squeamish. The conversation in the bar tends to revolve around few subjects and expletives are never deleted. The beer, Hadrian Gladiator or Whitbread Castle Eden, may come via the handpump or be served by gravity; either way it is a splendid pint. This place is a collector's item and, it must be repeated, not for those of a sensitive disposition.

The **Tynemouth Lodge**, a short walk from Tynemouth Metro, is the complete opposite of the Cumberland. The friendly landlord offers a selection of food and ale and a Sunday lunchtime bar snack selection you would have to go a long way to match. This is a favourite haunt of many of the inhabitants of Tyneside's coastal fringe and is nearly always busy without being overcrowded.

Another pub out of a similar mould is on North Shields

● Above North Shields fishquay is one of the best pubs on Tyneside, the Wooden Doll.

22   PUBS

Quayside. The **Chainlocker** has a mouthwatering selection of home-made meals at lunchtimes. There are normally two or three dishes which feature freshly caught local fish and are heartily recommended. The beers are good: Theakstons ales and usually one or two guests.

Across the road facing North Shields ferry terminal is the **Porthole**. This is a pub with a nautical theme. There are ropes and life belts and maritime paraphernalia everywhere including interesting signs on the toilet doors! Beer is varied with guest ales usually available.

Take the ferry to South Shields and you are within striking distance of the **Dolly Peel**. This is undoubtedly the jewel in the crown of South Shields pubs. A free house, it offers a wide range of ales. Many of these are often beers not usually available in the area. The pub has improved greatly recently and it is difficult to estimate its potential for future popularity.

In Gateshead the nearest pub to Newcastle is the **Queens Head** on Bottle Bank. Perched snugly beside the Tyne Bridge, this Bass outlet again offers excellent lunchtime fare and a choice of Bass or Stones. 10.30 closing can be a trap for the unwary and has often led to an embarrassing sprint back across the bridge to catch last orders on the Quayside.

Often overlooked, but not by those in the know, is the **Black Bull** in Blaydon. A bus or taxi along the Scotswood Road will no longer bring you to the races but rather to this superb Camerons pub with a charming landlady, excellent staff, delicious beer and, obviously, delighted customers. Two bars, one with a pool table which is not overly obtrusive and one with a real fire, provide a variety of comforts for any real ale drinker. A treat not to be missed.

On the return journey it is always worth looking in at Scotswood Road's Armstrong **Hydraulic Crane** – a name evoking memories of Newcastle's industrial past. Lunchtime meals dominate here but do not impinge on the quality of the beer.

Further afield is the **Jolly Fellows** at Ryton. This is a Whitbread pub serving Castle Eden and lunchtime meals in a pleasant atmosphere in the centre of an old village.

Finally, in Newcastle's northern suburb of Gosforth is the **Gosforth Hotel**. Simple meals are available in the bar on weekday lunchtimes. Beers are Tetley Bitter, Taylors Landlord, Marstons Pedigree and often a guest. Other bars open at weekends including a thriving disco.

A BIGG NIGHT OUT IN NEWCASTLE

The style. The look. The glamour. From Monument, along High Bridge and down the three Markets (the Bigg, the Cloth and the Groat) Newcastle is *the* place, a scene to see – and a site to be seen in.

They come by the bus and metro load, from as far as Teesside, Carlisle and Scotland, knowing that, for just a few hours, they will be centre stage: girls who look like models and dress like starlets, young men who walk cool and easy and know they are already heroes.

With over a dozen up-to-the-minute theme pubs and bars, the Markets become the centre of a great open air event. The atmosphere! The music! The excitement, the drama.

You'd think you were at one of the trendiest places in the world. And you are. These kids are the in-crowd, setting their own style, their own pace. They are already famous.

In an evening you can make your reputation. Remember the girl who wore the Robin Hood outfit made out of just one chamois leather? Remember the lad with the Porsche, who'd made a fortune in Saudi? Remember the night we all dressed up as nuns? Those were the days!

A night here can stay with you for the rest of your life. The romantic meeting, the traumatic breaking-up. True love and happiness? Or the one-night stand that will ruin your life!

Dangerous Liaisons or Rick's place in Casablanca. But this is the reality which Minogue, Madonna and the rest are trying to create. This is for real. In Newcastle we're living it!

But beware. It is for real. There are all sorts here: rough kids from tough areas, mean kids from bad homes – losers as well as heroes and heroines who are going to make it. And they are not to be gawped at or argued with. There are jerks who don't know what fun is, louts and lasses who drink themselves to Marbella on Tyne. And troublemakers who just want a fight. So take care, be streetwise.

And when Joe Robertson asks you what you're doing in his joint, say Dick Falkner sent you.

A GEORDIE PRINCESS. Where else could it be? On Tyneside even a hen night is different. Her friends dress the bride-to-be in a home-made hat and a bin-bag dress festooned with ribbons and streamers and messages of goodwill. And head for the Bigg Markets.

JOIN IN THE BIGG BUZZ

First get in the mood. Watch *Neighbours*. Phone your friends: you can't go on your own. Lads with lads, girls with girls – a roaming pack is best. Then all you need is...

THE LOOK

LASSES:
Have a few sessions on the sunbed. A tropical tan is a must if you want to meet the man of your dreams, but you could improvise with a fake tan. If you haven't got highlights, try a blonde rinse, and set your hair on heated rollers if it's not permed. Buy a luminous lycra dress from *Fiori* on High Bridge, or a pair of tight white shorts and a ballet top. Failing this, buy anything which shows more than it covers. You'll also need white stilettos and a bag big enough for your hairspray.

LADS:
Geordies of both sexes are very concerned about their appearance, and spend a lot of money on clothes, so if you're not prepared to make an effort you'll never fit in. Shop for designer trousers on High Bridge or in *Ricci*, and make sure they're well-ironed – you won't see a crease on Tyneside. A white shirt and silk tie (try *Next*) will be ideal, and some jazzy boxer shorts, expensive aftershave and wet gel will provide the finishing touch. Don't on any account wear a jacket, even if it's monkeys outside.

THE LOCATION

Take the Metro to Monument and follow the crowds down Grainger Street, turning left into the Bigg Market. Pick a pub – try Maceys, Balmbras or Presidents – and make a grand entrance.

THE TECHNIQUE

LASSES:
Perch yourself provocatively on a bar stool, and order a treble or a cocktail in a tall glass with plenty of ice and a straw. Begin to assess and discuss the talent, making numerous trips to the toilet so you can give the Jason Donovan lookalike a nod, a smile and a little flutter each time you pass by. At this stage, you may feel like joining in with the crowd by dancing round your handbag or singing the latest Stock, Aitken and Waterman at the top of your voice. By this time you'll have no problem forming a conga line to make your way to the next pub. Round the evening off at Julies or the Studio, or back to his place via the Kebab Centre.

LADS:
Get some serious drinking done first. Then, with a can of *Red Stripe, Grolsch* or any other overpriced imported beer in your hand, find the best position for looking at girls' legs and start discussing things like whether she's wearing any (hairspray of course), whether she's a goer, and if so, whether you're in with a chance. At the risk of getting the KB (knock back), try out some chat up lines. At closing time, head for the nearest Indian restaurant (*see separate section*) with the lads.

A gan doon the Bigg Market of a Freyder Neet cuz thez tottie aall awa, waall tu waall toosh man A'm tellin yuz...an' they're aall gaggin forrit.
● SID THE SEXIST (VIZ COMIC)

Balmbras (Cloth Market). Newcastle's first music hall, immortalised in the Geordie song *The Blaydon Races*, is now a massive disco-bar with its own DJ, flashing lights and mirrored walls.

Bar 42 (Hood St). This up-market sister pub to Whitley Bay's 42nd Street is open all day, with video screens, lighting effects, and a DJ on Sunday.

Berlins (Lower Westgate Rd). Smart cocktail bar named after Irving Berlin and fitted out in 1930s style. Typical customers are smart and over 30. Beer and lager prices are expensive here, but lower prices are charged for champagne and quality spirits.

Bewicks (Cloth Market). One of the smaller, more traditional style Bigg Market pubs, Bewicks has seats in the window which provide a good view of the goings-on outside.

Blackie Boy (Groat Market). A comfortable pub with an old fashioned theme comprising a genuine black-leaded range, numerous bookcases, leather sofas and armchairs, and an interesting large clock behind the bar. But it really is an old pub: it used to be the Groat Bar, and before that the Coffy Johnny.

Brahms & Liszt (Bigg Market). This Tetleys wine bar/disco is smart, trendy and comfortable.

Butlers Bar & Bistro (Nun St). This has a wine bar and disco downstairs and another disco upstairs for the younger set.

City Vaults (Bigg Market). A modern wine bar with a traditional feel about it. The City Vaults is a very old building and is said to be haunted: by a Roman soldier according to one story – or by a mysterious woman in white (sighted on Tuesday nights only!).

Dobsons (New Bridge St). This friendly up-market wine bar was named after Tyneside's famous architect John Dobson.

Eldon Grill (Grey St). This trendy up-market bar with videos is open 11am–11pm.

Fitzgeralds (Grey St). Recently refurbished, this smart bar appeals to an older crowd than the Bigg Market set. No DJ and no jukebox.

Legends (Grey St). Wine-bar/disco used by office workers and couples during the day. The bar is open plan with mirrors.

Maceys (Groat Market). One of the trendiest places in town! At lunchtime you'll find it full of yuppies executives knocking back lager with their hot beef sandwiches. But at night, particularly at weekends, it's the party atmosphere with loud music, bright lights and cans of Red Stripe. This is one of the smartest places to be seen at – if you've got the street cred! A spiral staircase takes you to the upper floor where you can relax in comfortable chesterfields.

Masters (St Nicholas St). A very busy city centre bar classed as up-market and lively, frequented by local office and Post Office staff (it used to be the Post Office Inn).

Nickys (Market St). Another city centre disco-type bar aimed at the younger age group with cut price cocktails most weekdays. The latest pop videos provide the entertainment.

Pineapple (Nun St). Owned by Camerons. A typical trendy, comfortable Newcastle pub with mixed clientele: smart young couples, shoppers, market workers. Disco Thursday and Sunday and singles club (Tues and Wed private).

Presidents (Cloth Market). Disco bar aimed at younger age group. The theme is past American presidents, pictures of whom adorn the walls. The staff wear red mini-skirts.

Ricks (Cloth Market). Trendy Tetleys cocktail bar in the former Pumphreys coffee shop.

Robinsons (Bigg Market). This all day wine-bar/café has a relaxed atmosphere during the day (no jukebox, just quiet background music). Meals are served till 5pm, and there's a small beer garden at the rear.

Turks (High Bridge). Wine bar popular with smart, trendy types.

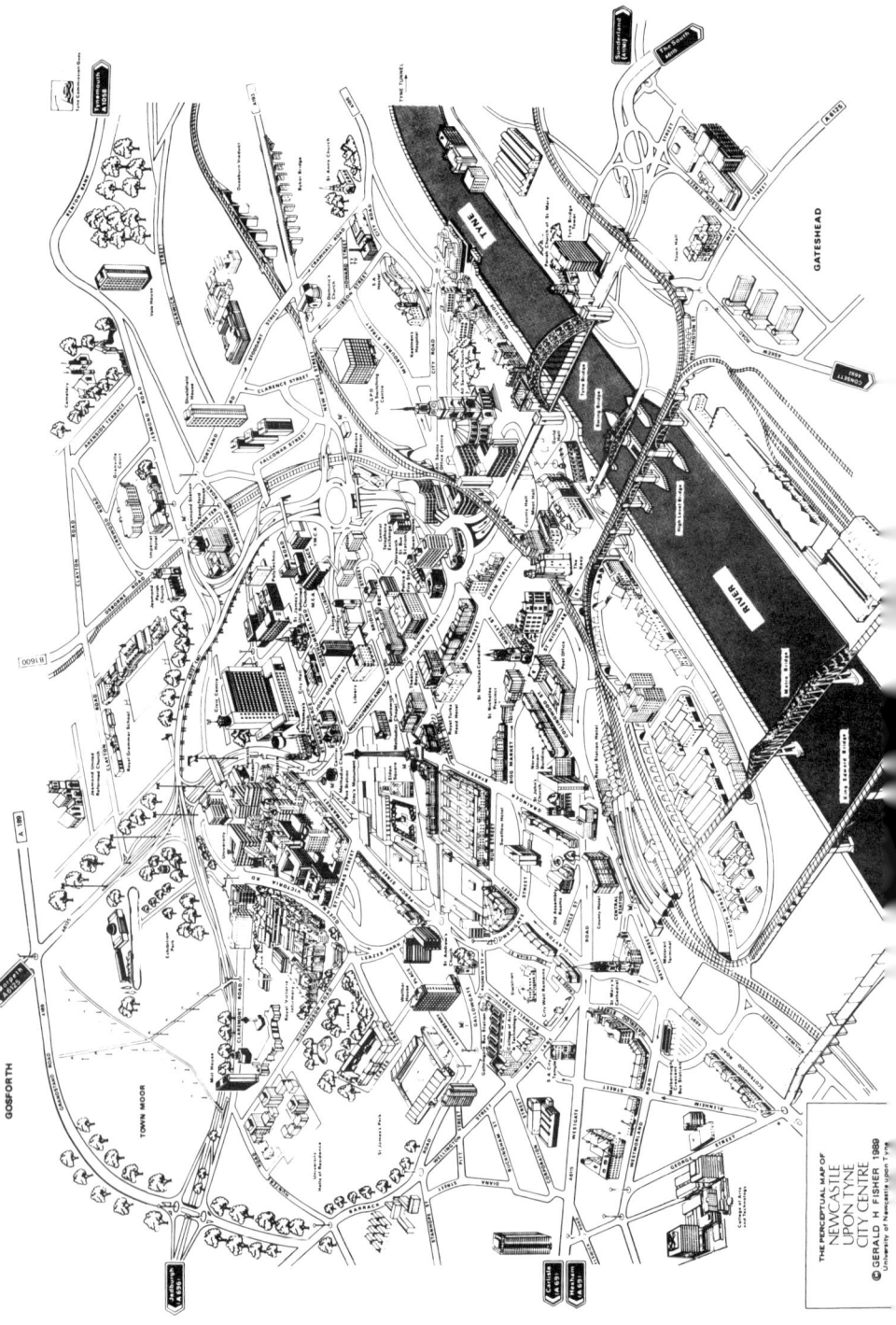

Alternatively...

If all the hustle and bustle of the Bigg Market is too much for you, there are still a few pubs left with a more traditional feel. Try the **Old George** and the **Duke of Wellington** – both good, old-fashioned pubs with a friendly atmosphere – or the **Bacchus**, which has stood up well against the tide of modernisation.

Near the Station are several pubs worth visiting. Don't

be misled by the outside of the **Dog and Parrot**. All is not what it seems. Done up like a dog's dinner and with some disconcerting video machines inside, this is in fact a pub for smart, discerning student-types, who form quite a cliquey in-crowd. But don't be put off by that! It's all very friendly. And they brew their own beer on the premises!

The **Forth** on Pink Lane is one of those traditional Geordie pubs where you feel instantly at home. Usually quiet and relaxed, it has the advantage of being a little bit tucked away, off the beaten track. Behind the station is the **Telegraph**, an absolute gem of a traditional Geordie pub used by the Post Office workers, who process mail 24 hours a day in the huge building opposite. Definitely a place to savour a bottle of brown.

But if you are into alternative music and cabaret, try the **Broken Doll** in Blenheim Street. It's one of those places which appear to be full of punks and weirdos, but once your eyes get used to the gloom, you realise it's no worse than the aliens' bar in Star Wars. Currently threatened by demolition, all those concerned about our environment should study these life forms before they disappear!

Adelphi (Shakespeare St). This traditional pub has a comfortable atmosphere, and is used by all kinds of people, including actors from the Theatre Royal.

Bacchus (High Bridge). Comfortable, traditional bar with a good range of meals at lunchtimes. Beers: Carlsberg, Black Label, McEwans, Murphys, Guinness, plus some cask-conditioned real ales.

The Broken Doll (Blenheim Street). Owned by Scottish & Newcastle, this pub reckons it's got the best looking bar staff in town. Live music, pool room, blues bar and very alternative cabaret. Beers: Theakstons, Guinness, Scrumpy, Slalom D.

Dog and Parrot (Clayton St West). The only pub brewery in Newcastle. Beers: Dog and Parrot Bitter, Wallop, Scotch, Cracker and Castle Eden. Food at lunchtimes.

Forth Hotel (Pink Lane, opposite Central Station). A traditional real ale pub with live music. Very friendly. Tommy Burns, former world heavyweight boxing champion, was a former landlord. Said to be the oldest trading pub in Newcastle. Beers: Tetley Bitter, Tetley Imperial, Tetley Falstaff, Taylors Landlord and Jennings Bitter. Food at lunchtime with good-sized portions and very reasonably priced.

Heroes (Clayton St West). Features pictures of heroes on the walls from all walks of life. Typical home-made food like mam used to make. Children welcome at lunchtimes. Open all day. Darts, pool, video bar.

Maxwells (Neville St). This bar has just been refurbished and is very comfortable, with chesterfields etc.

Formerly the Green Dolphin, it's now a friendly "country style" city centre pub with a faithful crowd of regulars. Used mainly by young people; early evening by office workers, lawyers, insurance businessmen. Food at lunchtimes: excellent value, fresh veg always served.

Newcastle Arms (St Andrews St). This traditional pub is described as typically northern, with a Tuesday night singalong and a quiz night on Wednesdays. The juke box has some great rock and roll records. Pub food is served at lunchtimes only at reasonable prices. Beers: Tetley, Burton Bitter, Castlemaine XXXX and Drybrough Scotch. The main types of customers are locals, students, office workers, travellers, and poetry supporters from Morden Tower on Friday nights.

Old George (Bigg Market). This old fashioned pub has an interesting history – Charles I was brought here after his surrender to the Scots, just before he was executed. The atmosphere is still traditional, with comfortable seats and wood panelling in the two rooms downstairs and one upstairs. A selection of real ales are available, with hot food and sandwiches at lunchtime. Regulars range from students to locals.

PUBS

Printers Pie (Pudding Chare, behind Thomson House). A traditional pub with a comfortable atmosphere, about to undergo a refurbishment programme. Snacks available and a good selection of beers and lagers. Typical daytime customers are printers, Post Office workers, reporters, etc.

Raffles (Pink Lane). A privately owned traditional and wine bar open all day every day with a mixed clientele. Beers: S&N, 80/- and Theakstons. Wide range of cocktails, a video jukebox and light bites at lunchtime.

Rosies Bar (Stowell St). Traditional image with Victorian/Edwardian theme, comfortable atmosphere, bar food. Used by businessmen, lawyers, bus travellers (Gallowgate), students and civil servants. Formerly the Northumberland Arms, then the Darn Crook, and now named after Rosie who still lives upstairs. They have a mynah bird in the bar; behind the bar are heads which move and there are bikes suspended from the ceiling. Beers: Tetleys, Jennings, XXXX, Addlestons.

Star (Westgate Rd). The manager offers two theories about the origins of the pub's name. The first is that the cellar of the pub was originally used for fighting rats (star backwards). The second is that everyone from the Beatles to the Rolling Stones and the Animals used to drink there when performing at the Majestic dance hall opposite (now a bingo hall). An old-fashioned pub, the Star has a jukebox, traditional pub grub and the usual Bass range of beers available in the two lounge bars. A mixed clientele of passing trade, businessmen, locals and Newcastle College people.

Duke of Wellington (High Bridge). This is a good city centre Bass pub with an unpretentious atmosphere. A good place for a relaxed pint and a bite to eat at lunchtimes, it livens up in the evenings, and is crammed full by 9pm.

Wilders (Carliol Sq, behind Worswick St bus station). A trendy wine bar open 11am – 11pm except Sundays. Beers: Harp, Becks, McEwans, Exhibition, Guinness. Also caters for small parties at reasonable cost.

Yates Wine Lodge (Neville St). Open all day, every day. A pub with a very busy atmosphere, with a singer on Tuesday and Wednesday evenings. It is a free house and sells special fortified wines brewed by Yates. Formerly the Victoria & Comet – in the days when it was used as the pub in the film *Get Carter*, when regulars taunted tough guy actor Michael Caine for ordering lager, then considered a ladies' drink. It's the first watering-hole confronting travellers emerging from Newcastle Central Station. The off licence at the front is also handy for anyone going off on a long rail journey (you'll pay much more on the train, with much less choice – and that's if you're lucky and the buffet isn't 'closed for stocktaking').

Heavy Stuff!

Now that the Haymarket pub itself, traditional haunt of Tyneside's bikers, has been pulled down, and the much lamented City Tavern has been converted into **Steppes**, Tyneside's not insignificant heavy metal contingent concentrates on the **Percy Arms**, the **Hotspur** and the **Farmers Rest**, before heading for a rock disco at the Mayfair on Friday and Saturday nights. **Trillians**, in Princess Square, despite a series of name changes (it used to be the Jubilee, and before that, The Man in the Moon) and new decor, is still very much a heavy haven and not for the faint-hearted.

Other pubs attracting a more mixed crowd but which still have heavy leanings are the **Northumberland Arms**, the **Market Tavern** and the **Three Bulls Heads**.

On the dormitory side of the campus, up Leazes Lane, is the famous **Trent House**, popular with students and well worth a visit for its Northern Soul jukebox. On the other side of Leazes Park is the **Belle Grove**, an interesting pub which manages to attract not just students but its traditional regulars as well as yuppies from the increasingly up-market Spital Tongues area just behind it.

A little further away is the **Spital House**, which still attracts the regulars who used to go there before it was rather disappointingly modernised, trading its fine gaunt, character for comfort!

On the other side of Richardson Road, the **North Terrace** is well worth a visit, despite its modernisations. The upstairs bar provides a homely communal lounge of respite from the spartan student flats in the Richardson Road complex. Back into town, on the doorstep of the university, in the Haymarket, is **Inventions**, an American-style theme pub attracting students and Geordies alike. It is full of pseudo-inventions and gadgets which actually turn out to be quite fun. We particularly like the Sinclair C5 being used as a plant-pot holder beside the loos!

A real knees-up for baby-boomers is **Sergeant Peppers**, where the DJ specialises in 60s and 70s hits. But if you're looking for an exotic theme like a Turkish harem, try **Steppes**, a lively pub on several levels, featuring a massive video screen. The harem ceiling is upstairs.

University Area

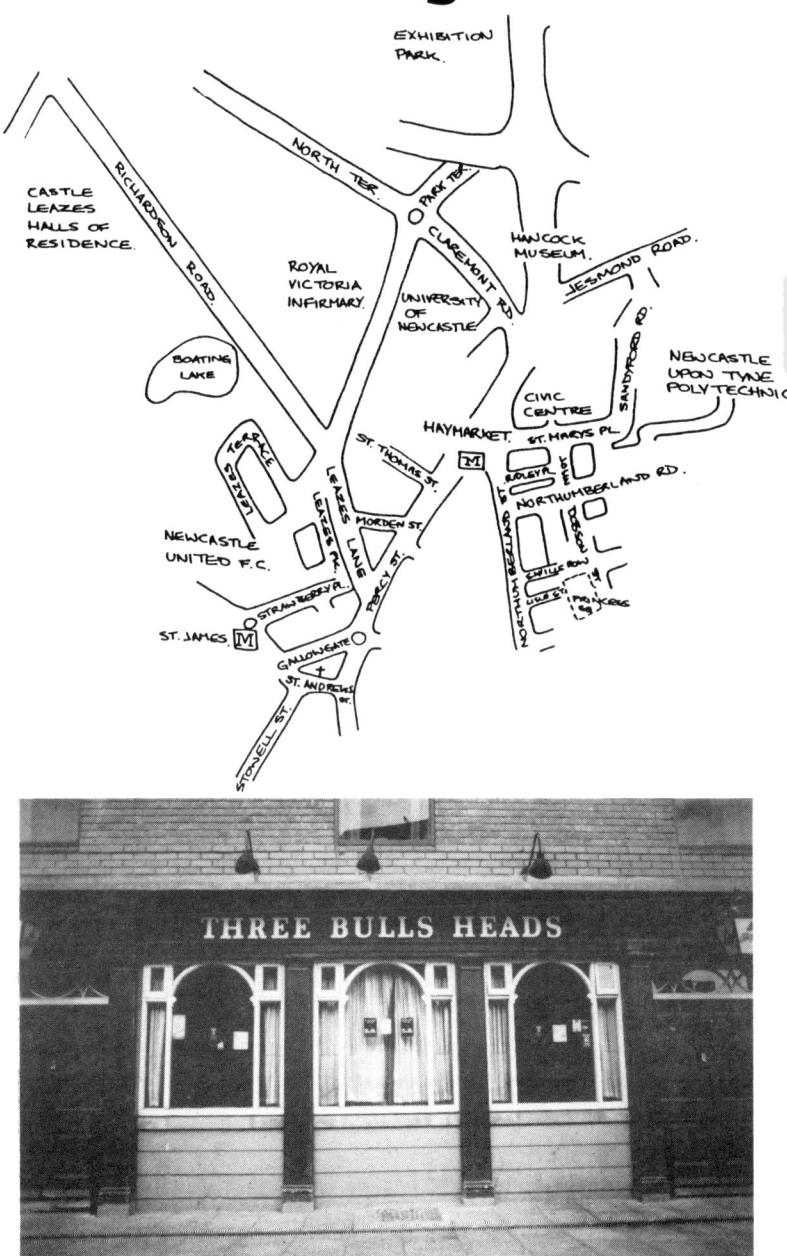

PUBS

Bourgognes (Eldon Sq). City pub and restaurant for shoppers and shopworkers, business people, office workers, etc. S&N house with Scotch, Exhibition, Cask 80/-, McEwans, etc. Food served from 12.00 – 7pm: good selection of main courses and sweets well prepared and well served at reasonable prices. At least three daily specials, sandwiches, hot beef sandwiches, coffee.

Concert Bar (Northumberland Rd). Basement bar in the City Hall full of students and office workers at lunchtimes; a good place for events posters. Heaving during rock concerts; understaffed for classical concerts and sometimes (unaccountably) closed by 9pm when the thirsty audience arrives for sustenance. There are tables and seats for first arrivals; latecomers have to perch on very uncomfortable tractor seats.

George & Dragon (Eldon Sq). Caters for everyone from bikers to trendies to pensioners, and all feel at home. Traditional English food served lunchtimes only; all meals under £2. Excellent selection of beers.

Inventions (Percy St). Theme pub with traditional decor but a rather unusual theme. As the name suggests, the pub is crammed full of strange and amusing inventions – some devised by eccentric TV personality Wilf Lunn (of *How* fame), others by people from the university. There's a moustache mirror, which helps you "try on" the moustache that suits you, a C5 used as a plant pot, clowns on bikes who ride the tightrope across the ceiling...and many more.

Popular with students, Civic Centre and office workers, nurses, lecturers, and actors from the nearby Playhouse. Barbecues are held in the summer on the patio at the back. Very good selection of beers including cask-conditioned ales, Timothy Taylors Landlord, Green beer from Denmark, peach and strawberry flavoured lagers and different guest beers each week. The pub's special drink is the *shooter*, a lethal mixture of two or three spirits to be downed in one from a shot glass.

Northumberland Arms (Eldon Sq). S&N pub catering for daytime shoppers, shop staff and office workers, with a comfortable lounge; on two levels. Serves hot food (traditional menu) and sandwiches until 7pm.

Sergeant Peppers (Vine Lane, off Northumberland St). Tucked away behind Ridley Place, Sergeant Peppers (formerly the Whistle Stop), as the name suggests, has a Beatles theme, with the resident DJ playing 50s, 60s and 70s hits seven nights a week. This is a great pub for a sing-along with a group of lively friends: your eyes will mist over as the resident DJ plays all your old Bay City Rollers, Slade, Abba and T Rex favourites. The DJ has even been known to offer the microphone to the more enthusiastic performers. There is a good choice of bar meals.

Sloanes (Hancock St, behind Civic Centre). The atmosphere at this wine bar/diner is relaxed and upmarket. It is a 'Garden within the City' and has won Northumbria & Newcastle In Bloom several times. Good selection of reasonably priced food ranging from large finger bun sandwich with help yourself salad to steak and kidney pie cooked in beer; wide range of beers and lagers.

Steppes (Northumberland Rd). The transformation of the City Tavern into the up-market and fashionable Steppes took place in 1987. Owners

S&N characterise it as a cafe-bar, and have given it a slogan to match the new image – 'the height of sophistication'. Open 11am – 11pm except on Sundays, the decor follows the current trend for the "traditional look" – wood and brass, and leather chesterfields. The multi-level bars and corner areas with comfortable sofas lend this huge pub a smart, continental atmosphere. During the day, the music is very much background for the daytime shoppers and businessmen, and children are welcome. In the evening, the largest video screen in the North East is lowered from the ceiling and the latest pop videos attract the younger, smarter crowd. With an interesting range of beers including Demon beer, the strongest pale ale in the world at £2.95 a bottle and Theakstons XB, food available all day, and jazz on Mondays and Wednesdays, Steppes has a lot to offer.

Strawberry Inn (Strawberry Lane). The manager's catchphrase for the pub is 'we sell, beer, tabs and a selection of crisps'. It is purposefully very basic in every way, and appeals to those students and other punters who like their pubs to be unpretentious. A real ale pub, it is very busy in the evenings, at weekends and before matches at St James's Park (across the road).

Three Bulls Heads (Percy St). Bass outlet, and a favourite student haunt, especially for agrics, medics and rugby players. Now wedged beneath part of Eldon Square, the Bulls used to be part of a rambling old Percy Street block including the Handyside Arcade and (upstairs) the famous Club-a-Go-Go, where the Animals played in the early 60s.

Trent House (Leazes Lane). Just down the road from the Strawberry, the Trent fills a gap for the "in crowd" of student drinkers who would rather be near their bus stops home to Fenham than down at the Quayside with the rest. It is always packed out and often has cheap beer promotions. A real ale pub, beers include 80/-, No.3, and Dixons. The music is particularly notable as the pub is run principally by a local club DJ, who knows not only his contemporary music scene well but has a good selection of revival music from the 50s, 60s and 70s. Popular with students and locals, especially at weekends and before matches at nearby St James's. Great atmosphere.

Trillians (Princess Sq, opposite Central Library). If you thought heavy metal was dead, you've obviously never set foot inside Trillians. Traditionally the home of the biker, Trillians, which used to be the Jubilee (and before that the Man in the Moon), is not the place to go for a quiet night out with your girlfriend or boyfriend. The atmosphere is hot and heavy, and the music loud. If you've got long hair, preferably dyed black and standing six inches from your head (goth) or blonde and layered like Status Quo (biker), skin-tight leopardskin trousers and a leather jacket, Trillians is the place for you.

PUBS 37

An Absolute Must!

After years of neglect, the Quayside is fast becoming Newcastle's most fashionable area, with new housing (for yuppies), a new courts complex – and millions of pounds worth of redevelopment in the offing. As the main artery of Tyneside, the river still has great magic and atmosphere. There are some fine old buildings, good traditional pubs and restaurants and some very good new ones as well. A stroll along the Quayside and a drink or a meal is an absolute must for anyone visiting the city. The newest, smartest Quayside bars are **Offshore 44** and **Hanrahans**. But if your tastes are more basic try the **Cooperage**, a little further along. This wonderful old building is now a great haunt for students and hippies with plenty of frayed leather and denim and a vigorous pool-table. For something a bit more relaxed and middle of the road, head back the other way, and try **Flynns**.

Just behind the Quayside, near the famous Fishermans Wharf restaurant, is the **Crown Posada**, a gem of a pub with a wonderfully relaxed atmosphere where beer swiller and snob will feel equally at home.

> The Crown Posada on the Quayside is a proper pub which has not been modernised and has no music apart from the odd appearance of old George, a resident of the Salvation Army who sometimes entertains on the mouth organ. Fine traditional beers, and the Murphys stout is excellent. The Fishermans Wharf nextdoor is an excellent fish restaurant with a large à la carte menu. The tables have lots of room. Excellent service, if a little pricey.
> ● TIM HEALY, ACTOR
> (AUF WIEDERSEHEN, PET)

Above the Quayside, the **Bridge Hotel** is another friendly pub with a good mix of regulars and heavy Real Ale leanings. But right along the other end of the Quayside, way up at St Lawrence, below Byker, is the **Free Trade Inn**. This is a favourite watering-hole for arty folk, media people, teachers, graduates, social workers, etc.

Quayside Area

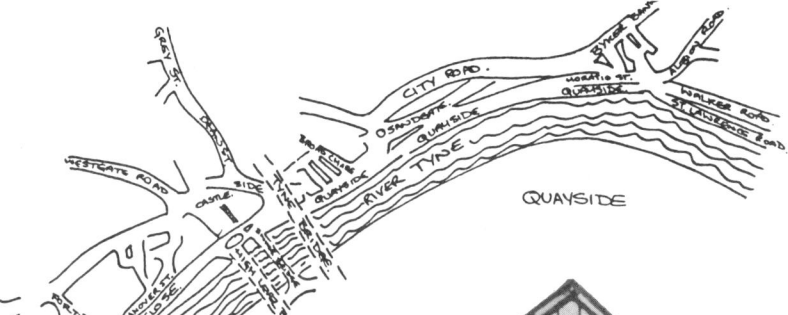

Baltic Tavern (Baltic Chambers, Quayside). This is two pubs side by side, one traditional, the other a tavern – one of the oldest pubs in Newcastle, dating back about 200 years, a welcoming pub with a choice of real and cask ales, wines and beers. They sum up their customers as a good mix. Food is served lunchtimes and evenings.

Barley Mow (Sandgate Hill, just below Tyne Tees). This is one of the most lively pubs in Newcastle and is almost exclusively a student and young persons hang-out. The jukebox in one bar is wide ranging and you can even bring your own discs to play! The bars are on various levels, and the most crowded is usually the one with a satellite pop music and video channel. The Mow (pronounced to rhyme with *cow*) sells several real ale beers including Tetley, Websters, Pedigree and Burtons. There is an excellent view of the Tyne from the beer garden, and if it's too cold to sit outside, there are two log fires in the quieter bar. Also a venue for gigs.

The Cooperage (The Close, Quayside). The Cooperage dates from the late 1390s and is a listed building. It looks quaint leaning out from all the other buildings, but is still very robust and has a disco till 2am upstairs on Friday and Saturday nights, with live music on alternate Thursdays. The building has stayed unchanged for years and the many tiny bars are all uneven in size and shape. It's a traditional public house, with a good selection of cask ales coupled with wholesome and traditional English food, e.g. bacon chop with a Scrumpy sauce and fresh vegetables. Private rooms also available catering for 20–200 (currently no charge for hire). Bar food is served until late upstairs.

Bridge Hotel (Castle Garth, next to High Level Bridge). This traditional pub is popular with newspaper reporters and students. There is a jazz club and folk club in the basement bar on Tuesday and Thursday nights. The legendary Bridge Folk Club was started up over 20 years ago by the High Level Ranters. Sandwiches only available. Beers: Theakstons, Tetley, Best Bitter, McEwans, and guest ales from all parts of the country.

Crown Posada (Side). This must be one of the few pubs in the whole of Newcastle that doesn't have a jukebox, so you can really have a conversation here! A very old and particularly handsome pub, although it is shaped like a corridor, or "two people deep from the bar". *Posada* is Spanish for tavern (the building was reputedly owned by a Spanish nobleman who kept his mistress there). It is a grade 2 listed building, with a magnificent moulded ceiling and two 18th century stained glass windows. It occasionally has excellent buskers, and appeals to students and locals alike, as well as to media men from the Quayside's advertising agencies. The atmosphere is comfortable except on Friday and Saturday nights when it is chocker. It is a friendly watering place, with much insulting banter and excellent beers: Timothy Taylor, Landlord, Hadrian Gladiator, Stones, Big Lamp Bitter, Murphys, and a different guest ale every week.

Egypt Cottage (City Rd). Popular with students, locals and media folk (and some TV stars!) from Tyne Tees Television next door. Rated as "student-trendy", but less cliquey than the nearby Barley Mow. The jukebox has some brilliant 50s and 60s music, and there's a quiet bar upstairs which few people seem to know about. Also real ale.

Flynns Bar Diner (Quayside). One of those modern pubs which for years was trying to find the right image and has now found it. A relaxed, low-key designer drinking house for those who don't want to be seen posing too hard. Theme based on film actor Errol Flynn, swashbuckling atmosphere. Large range of imported beers and wines from all over the world and many interesting cocktails. Fantastic views over river. Leather chesterfields in upstairs lounge. Occasional quiz nights. Beers: Castlemaine, Labatt, Hansa, Tetley, Murphys, Camerons, Timothy Taylor, draught ciders.

Free Trade Inn (St Lawrence Rd, below Byker). This pub makes a point of being very rough and ready: it appeals to the bearded and the bald, the denimed and the designer-stubbled. It's the trendy meeting place for eternal students and hippies, for poets, musicians, teachers, social workers and the Live Theatre mob. Noted for its highly individual jukebox (including blues, jazz and Van Morrison's *Brown-Eyed Girl*), its displays of forthcoming events

40   PUBS

posters (all the latest local gigs), and for the uninhibited graffiti in the loos. Also deafening live music or cabaret on Tuesday nights. Real ale and good views of the Tyne. Food served lunchtimes only. Beers: Theakstons, No.3, Becks, and low alcohol lagers and ciders, and the best kept Guinness in the North East; also a good selection of malts. Two cats complete the menagerie.

Hanrahans (Sandhill, Quayside). Like Offshore 44 opposite, this American-style bar diner in the Watergate Building is another place where smart wrinklies will not feel too out of place, but which is taken over by the young pace-setters at weekends. Plenty of Armani suits and Next outfits here. And they do food as well (see Restaurants section). It's packed so solidly on weekend evenings by Newcastle's Bright, Not Particularly Young Things that queues at the door are not uncommon. The long, curved bar-room is equally popular with early evening and lunchtime drinkers from the newly fashionable Quayside offices. Hanrahans has a separate restaurant whose menu follows the American theme of the bar.

● **The stylish bar at Hanrahans on the Quayside.**

Newcastle Arms (Akenside Hill, Quayside). Situated right under the Tyne Bridge, this is a comfortable pub – despite the outside appearance. Used by labourers and office workers during the day and mainly by students in the evenings. The beers include various real ales and imported lagers. Pictures of the local area are a prominent feature. Traditional English hot lunches – meat, potatoes & veg, and tasty Cumberland sausage sandwiches.

Offshore 44 (Quayside). Decked out like a smugglers' cave, a place where businessmen can feel as much at home as the young set. Offshore 44 achieved instant popularity with the oldest swingers in town, who also, incidentally, frequent Berlins, the posers' paradise on Lower Westgate Road, easily spotted by the ranks of Mercs and BMWs parked outside: don't forget your portable phone!

Red House (Quayside). Another traditional pub, hundreds of years old, and very popular with students, with a Friday night reggae disco upstairs. Seedy back room, but the front room has a warm atmosphere and attracts a good mix of people of all ages and types. As well as the function rooms, there's a restaurant upstairs.

Shieldfield

If the raucous exuberance of the City Centre is too much for you on a weekend, try heading out east to the gentler pubs of Shieldfield, just a short walk from the City Centre.

Just across Newcastle's Central Motorway is Shieldfield, a place with a cluster of pubs, which now attract a lot of customers from elsewhere in the City, particularly Jesmond and Heaton which have a dearth of good drinking places. From the town centre, you go up the steps at the Crest Hotel by the Oxford Galleries and come out across the walkways to Manors Metro and the new Warner Brothers multi-screen cinema centre.

The first pub you come to is **Joe Wilsons**, a traditional Tetleys pub with a 50s atmosphere and a small band of loyal customers. Next to it in Argyle Street is the **New Bridge**, another 50s pub but with a stronger atmosphere. These both tend to be used by locals.

To find the Shieldfield pubs, turn left down Falconer Street and follow the road round until you come to the **Queens Arms**. This is a nicely refurbished Matthew Brown pub, with a real fire, good beer and comfortable surroundings. It's fairly up-market and tends to attract graduates, businessmen, professional people and the discriminating drinker.

Go further and follow the road (Shieldfield St) round and you'll come to the **Globe**, a traditional Bass pub which has now become popular with artistic graphic designer and social worker types. Across the road from it is the less attractive (but less smoky!) traditional Geordie local, the **Shieldfield Inn**. But tucked away behind the shopping centre at the back of the Globe is the **Harrogate**, a nicely modernised traditional pub with a good bunch of regulars.

42   PUBS

Shields Road Byker

The best modern pub crawl on Tyneside

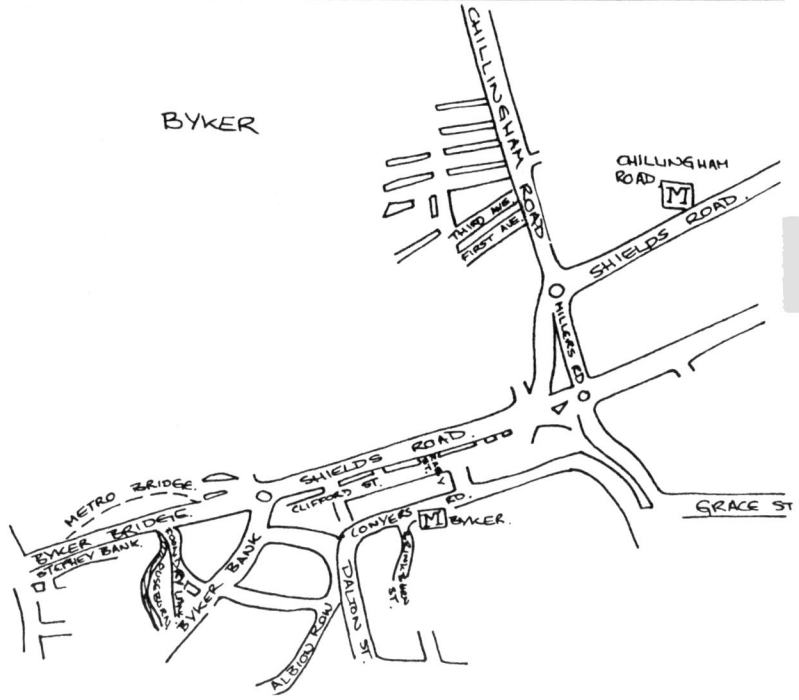

If you want a good, Geordie pub night-out or a chance to see what life on industrial Tyneside really used to be like, you can do no better than take a trip up Shields Road, Byker. Pubs on almost every corner – some of them scarcely changed in a decade. You can get to feel something of traditional Tyneside. Take the Metro out to Chillingham Road.

You emerge from the Metro near the end of Third Avenue opposite the **Chillingham**, a sadly modernised Tetleys pub only worth visiting because it is described by Tyneside novelist Jack Common as being the pub where, as a child, he used to sit outside watching his drink-sodden mother drown her sorrows with her cronies. Back over the railway bridge, you pass the shunting yards for NEI Parsons where Jack's father worked as an engine driver. At the roundabout you reach Shields Road proper: a little further up is the **Lord Clyde**. This once fine hotel is quiet and solid and has all the feel of the traditional pub. In spite of a little tarting up, some of the tables in the public bar are the same as they have been for decades. It has a timeless quality.

Across the road from there is the **Bluebell**, a rougher, tougher, fifties-modern place, heavy on polyurethaned plywood. The social life is based very much around the bar, the jukebox and the pool table. Just along from the Bluebell, almost in the shadow of the Byker Wall, is the **Glendale**, a Bass pub with a traditional look and a nice, pubby feel but actually quite modern and well fitted-out.

Back onto Shields Road, the **Grace Inn** on the corner of Robinson Street is an old-fashioned place. Head down the hill past **Jacksons**, an S&N pub full of brickwork and with large fitted carpets and disco lights. Fitted out only a few years ago to cash in on a trend, it now seems badly out of place. Further along is the **Raby**, one of Byker's best-known pubs, which was being refurbished as this guide went to press.

In pubs along Shields Road you can still see the old folk of Byker who were captured so well in Sirkka-Liisa Konttinen's book of photographs (taken when they were pulling down the terraced streets to build the Byker Wall): old people whose ancient love affairs, prejudices and battles still surface in the banter across the tables.

● **A traditional Byker night out: from Sirkka-Liisa Konttinen's acclaimed book *Byker* (Bloodaxe Books/AmberSide).**

On the corner of Brinkburn Street is **O'Briens**, a pub full of local people but this time a younger set. Formerly the Heaton Hotel, it looks better from the outside than inside. One of the mainstay pubs of Byker, on the corner of Dalton Street, is the **Butchers Arms**. Don't be put off by the garish signs on the outside: inside is the heart of a true Tyneside pub. Across the road the **Tap & Spile** looks like the traditional Geordie Byker pub but isn't. The interior is a bare boards, stripped pine and real ale job, with fine beers, attracting young up-market customers. Locals tend to avoid it ('We're not going in there, it's full of people from Jesmond').

Further down on the same side are the **Ford Arms** and **Baxters**, two pubs which have been tarted up in a disappointing, characterless way that seems to fall between the two stools, being not quite right for local people wanting a comfortable night out, nor sophisticated enough for the smart set wanting somewhere trendy. Across the roundabout, the **Plough** is better for a comfortable night out: an S&N pub in the shadow of Byker Wall whose residents it serves.

You are now on the edge of the Ouseburn. And it's well worth going down into the burn itself. And not just to see the bridges – the modern Metro bridge, the railway bridge, the road bridge and the tiny little brick bridge going across the stream itself. Beside the stream is the **Ship**, a traditional Whitbread pub that has mellowed and become a real ale pub with character. It's right opposite Byker City Farm, so at weekend lunchtimes and early evenings you often find parents bringing their children down to see the animals while they enjoy a pint. At the top of the valley on the Byker side is the **Cumberland Arms**. This is a real ale pub with a self-conscious Real Ale sign outside.

Jesmond Area

Jesmond is traditionally the Chelsea of Newcastle. The posh suburb that is so close to town it's now almost inner-city. It's arty, it's trendy, it's chic and it's also expensive: so much so that many of the large Victorian houses are being carved up into flats so that the bachelor boys and girls and trendy young couples and media people can afford them. The chicness has its advantages if only because discerning people know a thing or two about food and drink, and because they know how to complain the standard of goods and services in Jesmond is consistently high.

In the trendy Acorn Road shopping centre, you'll find greengrocers who know from bitter experience when avocados are ripe. In Jesmond you'll find butchers who won't raise their eyebrows when you ask for a Crown of Lamb: like Loughs in Holly Avenue West, where they'll not only do you a Guard of Honour, or a Northumberland Duck (not the bird but a shoulder of lamb shaped like one), but they'll also deliver it to your door.

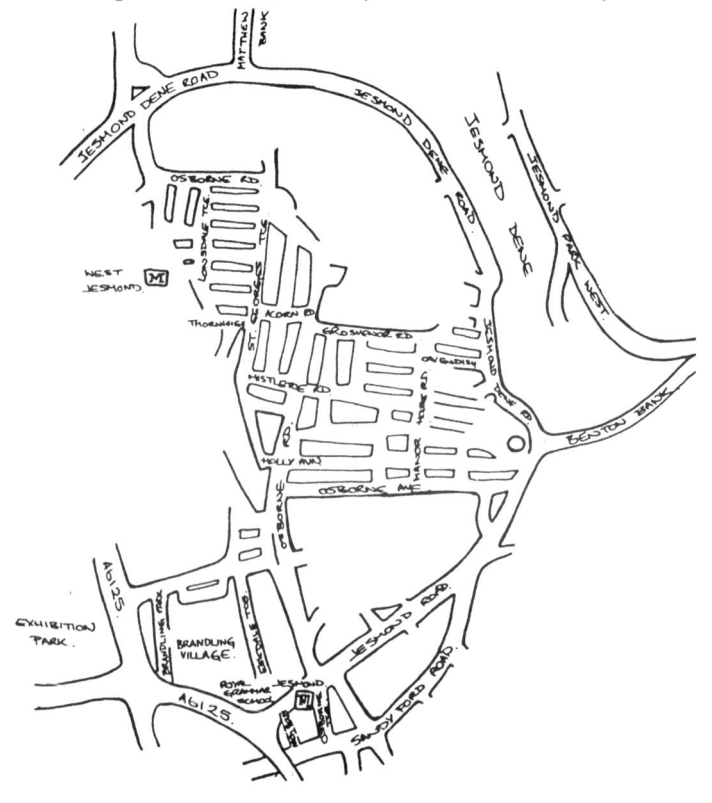

You'll also find two of the best Indian takeaways, the Alhelal Tandoori in Cavendish Road and the Jesmond Tandoori on Jesmond Road; and in South Gosforth an excellent Italian delicatessen selling fresh pasta, Italian cheeses and breads, good Chianti: Tavasso in Newlands Road. Another sign of the area's affluence is its many antique shops.

However, when it comes to pubs, the discriminating drinkers of Jesmond obviously prefer to stay at home with their mail order cases of wine from *The Observer*. The area is the victim of Quaker planning restrictions, for when Jesmond was built during Victoria's reign the city fathers were trying their damnedest to make Newcastle a prohibitionist city. Subsequently there are only a couple of drinking places in Jesmond itself and all the rest are scattered round the outskirts.

The **Lonsdale** at West Jesmond Metro Station is the only genuinely southern pub in Newcastle. Not only is the decor the epitome of a southern suburban pub, the accents too will beam you 300 miles to the south. What you won't find though is a pint of Watneys. The beer is mercifully northern. It's usually very full, particularly at weekends, and is popular with students and with the pop group Prefab Sprout (some Sprout members live round the corner); on Tuesday nights there's jazz upstairs with the resident band, the River City Jazzmen.

If you want something a little livelier, go to Jesmond's main thoroughfare Osborne Road and head for **Trotters**. Originally conceived as a trendy wine bar for yuppies, it still attracts hooray-henrys and rich kids in beach buggies, as well as a fair quota of bemused businessmen. It sometimes has live music, and is by and large fairly civilised though crowded, the glittering lights and expensive prices attracting sloanes of the predatory kind (sloanes with money *and* "class" tend to use the Brandling Arms).

Most Jesmondites head north, south or west to do their drinking. To the north the **Millstone** at South Gosforth offers a friendly atmosphere and an unforced naturalness you won't find at Trotters together with hearty pints of Bass. Across the road is the **Brandling Villa**, which is much more exciting on the inside than it looks from the outside, and just across the junction at the bottom is the **Victory**, a Scottish and Newcastle house, with an understandably loyal band of regulars.

To the south of Jesmond are two less attractive pubs which tend to be used by university students and graduates. The **Cradlewell** is the most studenty and has a reputation as a haunt for would-be gate-crashers trying to suss out where this weekend's big party is. But it does have the advantage of being large and caters for a wide range of customers. More comfortable but more crowded is the **Punchbowl**. It often seems as though half of Jesmond is crammed into its lounge bar. However, the public bar has managed to retain its traditional image, and you can have a pint or a game of darts there without getting drawn into a pretentious conversation at the bar.

To the west of Jesmond, tucked away between the Metro line and the Central Motorway is Brandling Village, an area with some expensive houses overlooking the Town Moor and Exhibition Park. There are two pubs tucked away behind them, the **Brandling Arms** and the **Collingwood**. Perhaps because they are tucked away they are popular with the young smart set, ex-RGS (Royal Grammar School) boys and ex-Church High girls, third year students and postgrads, real sloanes and student sloanes. A fair number of older people from Jesmond and Brandling Village use them too, and the Brandling has a dartboard, pool-table and dominoes.

More gimmicky is the **Carriage** set along the railway track, converted from the old Jesmond station, a real carriage and a rebuilt signal box (which houses a rather uninspiring ristorante). Despite its rather over-the-top British Railways memorabilia atmosphere and the fact that it attracts a lot of people on their way into town, it's not a bad place to stop off for a drink.

Heaton

For as long as most people can remember, Heaton has been the up-and-coming suburb of Newcastle. As the housing pressure on Jesmond has grown and prices have gone up and more houses have been converted to flats, the young couples have increasingly turned their eyes on Heaton. A lot of the houses have now been gentrified and signs of this creeping invasion are to be seen in the growing numbers of trendy shops on Chillingham Road and Heaton Road. One interesting phenomenon is Heaton Hall Road where an astonishing number of bric-a-brac and not-quite-antique shops seem to make a reasonable profit clearing the houses of Heaton's erstwhile generation once they die or move into old people's homes, then selling the contents back to the new younger generation as they move into the same houses.

Heaton is another area with virtually no pubs of its own. However, it does boast the **Corner House**. Despite being garishly modernised in a flashy 80s style, which makes it look like a huge terrarium, it still manages to be the best live music venue in the region with an unrivalled reputation for its jazz nights. You will also find food (their Sunday dinners are very good value), a good mix of people, and in the summer you can sit outside and inhale the fumes from all the traffic coming in on the Coast Road.

Down Heaton Park into the dene in Sandyford you will find the **Bluebell** at Jesmond Vale, a disappointingly modern pub in a delightful setting. It gives a warm enough welcome despite being rather crowded, and has a garden with tables behind which is popular with families and gardeners from the neighbouring allotments at weekends. Alternatively the Heaton drabbies head for the Globe at Shieldfield, while the yuppies go to the Queens Arms or the Tap & Spile in Byker.

Whitley Bay

Out at the coast on summer evenings Whitley Bay comes into its own with a whole range of bars along the seafront for the young and beautiful of Tyneside. There is even a bar – **Dunes** – almost on the sand where you can sit sipping cocktails watching the boats skim over the waves and the water skiers doing their stuff.

To the north of Spanish City is the wonderfully modernised **Berkeley Tavern**. It looks trendy enough – where people who buy their clothes from Marks and Spencers won't feel too much out of place – but it's south of the Spanish City funfair and amusement arcades that the real scene begins, and the further south you go the trendier it becomes.

The Tetley pub **Vagabonds** looks trendy enough, aimed at giving a comfortable drink to holidaymakers staying in the many hotels. Across the little green, the Scottish & Newcastle pub **The Avenue** looks trendier and is smartly done out in a bright pseudo-fifties style of both chrome and neon lights. When our researcher called the music was heavy metal and the clientele very well mixed. On the next block there are hotels with ballrooms that are now used for disco dancing. These too are aimed mainly at the holiday makers.

It's south of the Golden Nugget at Burnside Lodge that the real excitement begins. Up South Parade is the **Rex Hotel,** together with a string of disco bars ranging from **42nd Street** with its banks of video screens and the sophisticated **Eezy Street**, small hotel bars and even a men's Catholic club. Although the emphasis at

PUBS

places like the **Olive Grove** is on loud music, flashing lights, the maximum of excitement, you find plenty of older people here, and if you're still looking for the **Dunes** bar, cross over to the seafront and look to your left. It's down on the lower promenade, right above the sea at high tide. In the next street south you will find **Idols** on the Esplanade. A popular disco bar, its nightclub atmosphere is partly generated by the fact that the bar staff are scantily clad in torn denim shorts and swimsuits. As you might expect, with so much stimulation the clientele tend to be a little longer in the tooth as they sit in the bars with their banks of video screens.

Locals tend to use pubs away from the front like the **Avenue** in Park Avenue, the **Victoria** in Whitley Road, or the **Bay Hotel** overlooking Cullercoats Bay, which used to be Lord Huddlestone's house. The Bay has a carvery and a restaurant with English and French cuisine; it has disco and cabaret nights, and rooms used more by people visiting the area on business than by holidaymakers. There's also a pool room, and the bars offer cocktails as well as a range of beers including Theakstons. The Victoria is a friendly pub open all day, with a singer on Thursday nights; the lounge is up-market, the public bar traditional, and the beers include Tetley and Pedigree.

Up the Coast

When you're tired of city pubs, try heading north out of Whitley Bay up along the coast towards St Mary's Lighthouse and beyond.

The first pub you pass is a free house called the **Briar Dene** remarkable for its huge stuffed lion and its cavernous interior. This is a rather large, loud sort of place, so give it a miss if you're wanting something quiet and head on up to the **Seaton Delaval Arms**, a small traditional sort of Geordie pub with a comfortable lounge and friendly bar. Its main advantage for the daytime visitor is that it's just a short cliff-top stroll from there to St Mary's Island. If it's low tide you can take the short walk across the causeway and have a wander round the lighthouse.

A little further on up the coast road is Seaton Sluice itself. Turn right at the fish and chip shop and you will see on your right a fairly unremarkable looking Vaux pub called the **Waterford Arms**. In fact this is a superb fish and chip pub and if that sounds odd you'll be even more surprised if you try it. The good beers and the very comfortable surroundings are complemented by the most amazing fish and chip suppers: the portions are enormous. If the small is quite large, the medium size is more than most people can handle, and the large is called Whale and Chips. They welcome children and even have some toys and things for them to play with before 9pm, but it gets very crowded early evening, especially at weekends.

Further on along the Sluice is the **Kings Arms**, a nice stone-built Scottish and Newcastle pub with a traditional feel which has been well modernised and unspoilt by the smartening up. It has a hearty atmosphere, especially at weekends, and a good mix of regular customers. Afterwards you can take a walk down to the Sluice and also take a look at the Octagon, a curious many-sided building known to the cognoscenti as Vanbrugh's After Dinner Thought – said to have been built by the great architect after he'd finished work on nearby Seaton Delaval Hall.

Further on up the Coast Road on your left at the other side of the Sluice is the **Melton Constable**, is a self-contained pub which has been well modernised and has a couple of tables on the outside to take advantage of the good view over the Sluice on fine days.

Half a mile or so up the road is the **Astley Arms**, named after the great local family from Seaton Delaval Hall, with their regalia and coats of arms on the walls. It's a thriving Whitbread pub which also does meals: very nice in a below-decks lounge bar style, and a comfortable place to have a meal and a night out opposite the dunes.

PUBS   53

Tynemouth

Tynemouth has always been popular with Newcastle folk wanting a summer night out. Partly it's the atmosphere of the wide main street which runs down to the Priory on the seafront and partly the fact that there are some good traditional drinking places, as well as some passable restaurants and an excellent fish and chip shop. An elegance about Tynemouth often surprises visitors which is typified by nice traditional pubs like the **Cumberland Arms**, with its attractive stained glass windows and rather contrived nautical atmosphere, and the genuinely characterful **Salutation Inn** which offers Whitbread ales, a quaint olde worlde atmosphere, and an appetising lunchtime fish menu.

Across the road is the Scottish & Newcastle **Turks Head**, a fine traditional Geordie pub, a real local for locals. With its cliff-top vantage point right beside the Priory, the Bass pub the **Gibraltar Rock** could be a real winner, but it's been rather spoilt with a garish cocktail room atmosphere; and its development as a carvery restaurant means it's now disappointing both as a pub and as a restaurant.

Newcastle revellers traditionally round off their night off in Tynemouth with a visit to one of the town's restaurants like the Gate of India or the Rawalpindi Tandoori. If you want a good fish restaurant, try Marshalls: it may not look like much but the fish and chips are excellent.

> My favourite pubs are the Wooden Doll (good beer, good crack) and the Chain Locker (good beer, good food) at North Shields, and in Newcastle, the Duke of Wellington, Bacchus, Bridge and Egypt Cottage (all good beer), the Crown Posada (best beer in the city), and the Newcastle Playhouse (good live music most nights). The restaurants I like are Café Procope (informal atmosphere with an interesting selection of food and foreign beers), Chi-Chi's at the MetroCentre (*authentic* Mexican food), Sachins (the **best** Indian restaurant on Tyneside), and Lady Eleanors at North Shields.
> ● ALAN HULL, MUSICIAN (LINDISFARNE)

North Shields

All along the River Tyne you can see the renaissance going on as the old Victorian yards and warehouses are either taken over by new companies and modernised or turned into offices and flats. A few years ago the words North Shields Fish Quay would have conjured up a rather drab and depressing image. Apart from the boats, fish and kipper curing sheds, there was an air of dereliction and the most notorious pub was one mainly known for drunken brawls and prostitutes and nicknamed The Jungle.

Nowadays there is a whole new atmosphere along the waterfront. The boats are still there and the smell of fish, but along the Quayside the pubs have been smartened up, and above them on the banks of the river old warehouses are being turned into luxury flats and new houses are being built.

At the far end of the Quayside away from the sea is the **Chainlocker**, a trendy Quayside Websters pub for Real Ale types. It has a good atmosphere with occasional live music and good beers. It's almost right opposite the landing of the Tyne Ferry which takes passengers across to South Shields. Further up is the **Porthole**, a very good, over-the-top, 50s-style pub with a strong ship theme and a good range of real ale, and with jazz on Monday and Tuesday nights. It also has a good selection of low priced meals, including kebabs at £2.50 and veal cordon-bleu for £4.95. Despite the nautical theme, this is a very nice pub to drink in, with its Theakstons beer and friendly bar staff.

Further along is **Wharfs**, a new Tetley establishment right on the wharf, a lager and restaurant sort of place with a somewhat manufactured atmosphere. After that you come to the **Low Lights Tavern**, a traditional Scottish and Newcastle which was there long before the yuppies moved in. It is named after the low light, one of two lights, one at the bottom of the bank and one at the top, which was used in the old days to guide ships into harbour.

Go up the hill and turn to your left and you'll come to the **Wooden Doll**, built in 1794 and named after the legendary Wooden Dolly, a copy of which stands in North Shields' Northumberland Square. This highly recommended pub has recently been extensively modernised, and is now extremely comfortable and inviting. It is arguably the best pub on Tyneside; apart from wonderful views, excellent beers and good food, it now boasts live music every night. There's also a good mix of customers, and the only thing to be said against it is that it's perhaps a little too smooth, a little bit too respectable.

Tucked away down by the river cranes on Appleby Street is a pub that has undergone an unusual reversal, the **New Clarendon**, which is owned by Amber Films, who use it as a television film set. When Amber took it over, they ripped out all the plastic and formica and turned it back into a traditional Geordie local. Now you can enjoy a singalong with the pianist and the pub's regulars on Friday, Saturday and Sunday nights.

Just out of North Shields are two other pubs worth visiting. The **Cannon Inn** on the New Coast Road serves lunches and evening meals, and has a beer garden and pool room. Open all day, the **Tynemouth Lodge** on Tynemouth Road is one of the best real ale pubs on Tyneside, with beers including Theakstons, Marstons, Wards and Belhaven.

On Burdon Main Row the **Wolsington House** is used by dock workers and ships' crews, and has live music every night. A similar pub in nearby Wallsend is the **Ship in the Hole** next to Swan Hunters, right under the bows of the giant vessel currently being built by the shipyard workers who use the pub at lunchtimes. In the evenings it's taken over by a mixture of pool-playing locals, North Tyneside drabbies and heavy metal freaks (whose thundering bands sometimes take the place over!).

Gateshead

Azure Blue (Eastbourne Ave, Gateshead). Modern, local pub with "friendly" bar staff. Occasional Saturday night discos, trivia quiz on Wednesdays. Down-to-earth bar, reasonably priced drinks. All types of customers ranging from students to families.

Fiddlers Three (Albion St, Windy Nook, Felling). Traditional S&N pub. Bar snacks lunchtimes and evenings, with an extensive, interesting menu; special requests (e.g. vegetarian) catered for if possible. Good range of beers. Wednesday is jazz night; Monday, quiz night.

Lakeside Inn (East Fellgate Farm, Leam Lane). Very friendly traditional bar with a comfortable atmosphere, set in seven acres of land including two large lakes used for coarse and trout fishing. They have recently opened a new conservatory. The food is first class with a good and varied menu.

Lambton Arms (Eighton Banks, Low Fell). This traditional bar is about 140 years old; it used to be the Engine Inn. It has a comfortable lounge bar and is used by white collar workers from the Washington Trading Estate. Children are welcome at lunchtimes. Beers include Whitbread Best Scotch, Trophy, Castle Eden. A good range of meals and they cater for vegetarians.

Moon & Sixpence (High St, Gateshead). This trendy pub has a 60s disco on Mondays, and live entertainment on Thursdays. It is said to have a ghost which bangs the cellar door and slaps the barman on the face when he's asleep.

Old Fox (Felling). This is a traditional Websters pub with friendly people who create a warm and welcome atmosphere. Various music and quiz nights; also darts, dominoes, pool. Reasonably priced lunches; bed and breakfast also available at £10 a night. Beers: Yorkshire Bitter, Websters, Guinness, Drybroughs Scotch, Pennine Bitter.

Ship Inn (Eighton Banks, Low Fell). Originally an ale house and tobacco and liquor store, this horseshoe-shaped Vaux inn is decked out with sailing ship pictures and models. One section of the pub is marked off as a no smoking zone, and outside are tables and a children's play area. There are real ales as well as Vaux beers (Samson!). The excellent meals come with a choice of fresh veg or a lavish help-yourself salad: specials like home-made beef casserole, home-made ham, cheese & mushroom pie; the captain's table (meat dishes); turkey kievs stuffed with cheese and garlic...

Wheatsheaf (Carlisle Street, Felling). Award-winning real ale pub, one of a handful on Tyneside supplied by Newcastle's Big Lamp brewery. Very friendly, and great for quiet out of town drink. There's folk music on Tuesday nights, and at other times too when the musical landlord gets together with other Big Lamp Irish folkies.

Out of Town

Balancing Eel (Ocean Rd, South Shields). One of the most popular wine bars in Shields, with resident DJs four nights a week and a quiz night on Wednesdays. The food is reasonably priced: e.g. prawn salad, £1.50, sausage & chips, 99p. Beers: Scotch, Guinness, Samson, canned beers & lagers; plus a variety of cocktails. Children welcome until 6pm.

Beehive (Hartley Lane, Earsdon, Whitley Bay). An old oak-beamed pub with a beer garden and a real fire; now 260 years old, it is a listed building and has been a pub for 120 years, and some locals have been regulars here for over 40 years. Darts and dominoes are available, and food is served at lunchtimes and in the evening: pie and chips, scampi, chicken, fish, etc, in the £1.20–£2.55 price range. Open: 11am–3pm & 6–11pm.

Blackbird Inn (Ponteland). This pub is 400 years old and stands on the site of a peace treaty signed between the Scots and the English in the 13th century. It has three bedrooms and four bars and offers a good choice of bar food. Opposite the pub is St Mary's Church, and the two buildings are linked by an underground tunnel. The pub garden is very popular in the summer.

Black Bull (Bridge Street, Blaydon). Traditional real ale pub with strong emphasis on good conversation, live music and other forms of live entertainment. Folk night Mondays, Quiz night Tuesdays, Jazz Thursdays and regular "one-off" events such as poetry, storytelling, Irish nights, etc. Cask beers: Camerons Strongarm, Premium, Trad. Bitter, Everards. Keg beers: Camerons Crown, Stowford Press Cider, Guinness. Children welcome afternoons and early evening.

Black Bull Inn (Middle Street, Corbridge). An old 17th century coaching inn offering a varied selection of meals lunchtimes and evenings at reasonable prices. Opening

> My favourite pubs are the Swinburne Arms at Stamfordham (small and nice), the Waggon at Belsay (big but relaxing) and the Falcon at Prudhoe. For fish and chips I go to the Quayside at North Shields. The Royal Derwent Hotel at Consett is good, and Greys Club is always lively.
> ● JACKIE CHARLTON, FOOTBALLER

PUBS

times vary according to time of year. Beers: Trophy, Scotch, Castle Eden, Murphy, Guinness, guest real ales.

Bowes Incline (Northside, Birtley). This pub has all day opening except on Sundays. They offer reasonably priced food evenings and lunchtimes, including Sunday lunch at £3.95. Thursday is quiz night. Beers: Stones, ELB, Bass, Stones Cask and real ale.

The Courtyard (Scotswood Rd, Newcastle). Traditional pub used by office workers and shoppers at lunchtime and by gays during the evenings. Cabaret on Thursday nights, and a women only night every Tuesday and the last Friday in the month.

Diamond Inn (Ponteland). A traditional S&N pub with all day opening. They have a quiz night on Sundays, and ski club and pony club nights on alternate Tuesdays. Beers: Scotch, Exhibition, 80/-, Becks, Theakstons, Guinness. Food available lunchtimes only.

Harbour Lights (Laws Rd, South Shields). This Bass pub is firstly a local and secondly an interesting pub due to its fabulous situation overlooking the Tyne river and harbour. Although not an official stopping point on the Catherine Cookson trail, it is on the route and has the best view of the coast. It has a singalong on Sunday nights and quiz night on Thursdays. Beers: Stones, Bass Best Scotch, Bass Light, Tennants, Guinness. Food available at lunchtimes.

Highlander (Higham Dykes, Belsay, Northumberland). Pub/restaurant run by David Swalwell in an olde worlde building which used to be a farmhouse. It has a courtyard and barns where barbecues are held if booked in advance. There's an à la carte menu in the restaurant, and a bar menu of home-cooked dishes which changes daily including traditional English dishes such as mince & dumplings and steak & kidney pie. Grills are served in the evening. There's no jukebox and no background music!

Jolly Fellows (Ryton). Village pub which used to be a coaching house; the stables are still under the pub cellar. It has its own darts team, pool team, leek club and football team.

Kicking Cuddy Inn (Durham Rd, Coxhoe). Pub with live entertainment on Fridays, folk on Sundays and discos once a month. Its history is linked with its name: it was originally a hotel used by horse-traders from all over Co. Durham. Meals served evenings and lunchtimes, with barbecue facilities in the beer garden; also has Shove Ha'penny and Scalextric cars.

Lion & Lamb (Horsley, Northumberland). A coaching inn built in the early 18th century, this is now a country pub and restaurant, a recent 'Wine Pub of the Year' winner. The bar is in the old stables, and has all kinds of wines as well as a selection of real ales.

Marquis of Granby (Streetgate, Sunniside). Homely country pub with a log fire. A singer entertains on Sunday nights and families are welcome at all times. Although this pub is in the middle of nowhere it is well worth a visit.

Mill (Blackhall Mill). Situated in a famous walking area within 5 minutes of the Derwent Walk. Beers: Stones, Labatts, Everards, Trad. Bitter, Dog.

Miners Arms (Acomb, Northumberland). Built in 1745, this village inn near Hadrians Wall (just off the A68) has an excellent selection of meals and real ale beers. The beers include the Miners Arms' 'Own Ale', Morrells, Federation, Murphys, Fosters, and guest real ales. They cater for vegetarians and produce regional dishes to go with the guest ales of the week, with meals served in the dining room or in the lounge in front of the log fire. Children welcome until 8pm.

Ship and Royal (Ocean Rd, South Shields). This traditional Tetley bar is friendly and comfortable, used by young Shields trendies and older locals. Although this is a town centre pub, it claims that its faithful regulars give it the feel a country pub in a small village. Discos on Friday and Saturday nights upstairs. Good selection of meals cooked in their own kitchens. Children welcome at lunchtime in the restaurant.

Top House (Marlow St, Blyth). Traditional local open all day except Sundays, with jazz and quiz nights. Beers: Theakstons, Slalom, McEwans, Guinness, Murphys.

Victoria Inn (Fatfield, Washington). Bass pub with pool room, beer garden and quiz nights. Beers: Stones, Scotch, Tennants Extra. Children welcome at lunchtimes when food is available.

With Chinese food we're spoilt for choice. My current favourite is the Dragon House (intimate and with excellent crispy duck!). Sachins is one of many excellent Indian restaurants: the subtlety of Punjabi cooking here is particularly attractive. For fish, the Fishermans Lodge and Fishermans Wharf are unbeatable for those in expansive mood – unbeatable Dover sole and halibut. 21 Queen Street has a most attractive decor and beautifully presented food, from intriguing appetisers like French Bean Vinaigrette, main courses with exquisitely cooked and presented vegetables, to breathtaking sweets which tempt me too much for my own good! For lunchtime specials, Café Procope has an enterprising range of dishes including some good vegetarian items and with some exotic beers. One-Eyed Jacks (formerly in High Bridge, now at Pilgrim Street) does Tex-Mex food: light, spicy and enjoyable, in spite of being good for you.
● **JEREMY BEECHAM**
   LEADER, NEWCASTLE CITY COUNCIL

RESTAURANTS

One of the joys of Tyneside is the sheer diversity of its restaurants.

At one end of the scale there are very cheap places with friendly staff and bags of atmosphere where almost anyone can afford to become a regular, and at the other, there are superb English, French and Chinese and Asian restaurants with top rate food and service that are hard to beat anywhere in the country.

The best restaurants may *seem* pricey... We once apologised to some visitors from London for choosing a restaurant which we thought was a shade over-priced. Their reaction was: 'Do you have any idea what we normally pay for this sort of quality?'

The great thing is that you are as likely to have a memorable and enjoyable meal in a cheap chaotic bistro or curryhouse as you are in one of the top restaurants.

A couple of thoughts, though. Be wary about where you eat after closing time: some places do fill up with rowdy louts. And if you do get a poor meal, *don't* make a scene (or everyone'll want one!) – but *do* tell the manager. And if you don't get the right response, write and tell us!

Tyneside, Where's the Buzz **was compiled from a wide range of reports from over a dozen anonymous researchers, who regularly use the pubs, restaurants and other facilities listed as paying customers.**

Traditional

FISHERMANS LODGE
Jesmond Dene, Newcastle.
☎281 3281.
Top class restaurant, one of the best in the north of England, opened in 1979 in the former town residence of Lord Armstrong. They specialise in seafood (fresh daily from North Shields fish quay), with dishes including braised monkfish with saffron, baked Tweed salmon in pastry, and Surf and Turf (beef fillet grilled with a half lobster and garlic). Other specialities include Northumbrian lamb, duck breasts and game.

Owners Franco and Pamela Cetoloni have trained some of the region's top chefs. 'No, no, we're not here to insist on formal diners,' say the Cetolonis, 'We want our clients to wear whatever they feel happiest in.' The chef once made a meal costing more than £100. 'But,' explains Franco, 'it was for a man with a guest who had just won a motoring society's salesman competition. They started with lobster and didn't move downwards from that!' Franco's own favourite dish on the menu is the Dover sole. Lunch, Mon – Fri; dinner, Mon – Sat; closed on Sundays.

FISHERMANS WHARF
Quayside, Newcastle. ☎232 1057.
Top class fish restaurant which also produces some quite excellent meat dishes. It's a small, wood-panelled restaurant with an upstairs bar area overlooking the tables: rather formal, but with good, properly cooked food. There is a good sweet selection presented not as a menu but laid out on a large tray so you can see what you are actually choosing; the wine list is fairly extensive but pricey. A meal here can prove very expensive, and if you're going to pay out for a really special meal it makes sense to go for the seafood.

The Fishermans Wharf (once a bank and still feeling a bit like it) used to be the sister restaurant of the Fishermans Lodge (see above), but the Cetolonis sold it to their own head chef, Simon Tennet, who has kept it going in the same style. His chef is Douglas E. Jordan: 'He's a wonderful chef; I work very well with him.' Fixed price meals at lunchtime cost £11.50 and among the exciting starters offered the day we called was salmon mousse stuffed with various attractive things. A la carte choices range from £3.60 to £6.70, with main courses priced from £7.50 to £18.50. Lunch, Mon – Fri; dinner, Mon – Sat; closed on Sundays.

GOSFORTH PARK HOTEL
High Gosforth Park. ☎236 4111.
The menu is large and extravagant, but the manager says his chefs will cook *whatever* a customer wants, as long as they have the ingredients: 'But no elephant,' he pleads, 'We do not have elephants.' Every week the chef creates a "special menu" for £25, always intriguing, but attracting anything from one to 30 diners

per week. Fixed-price set lunches, £12.50. Open: 12.30 – 2.40pm & 7 – 10.30pm (last orders).

HARVEYS OF ST JAMES
St James Park, Newcastle.
☎222 1860.

A swish complex of restaurant and banqueting suites inside the Milburn stand at St James's Park, named after Newcastle United football legend Joe Harvey: a massive place, like a hotel without bedrooms. The accent here is on luxury: Royal Doulton china, damask tablecloths, fine cut glassware, etc. Open all week and available for conference bookings, weddings and other occasions in several different banqueting rooms, from eight to 350 people. Yet, for such surroundings, and with the quality of food – with ingredients flown in fresh from Paris – Harveys is not overpriced. Match days are popular: there is a set lunch at around £10 per head, a set evening meal at around £12.50 and an à la carte menu where the sky's the limit. The main type of food served is French: e.g. *starter,* trout mousse in an envelope of leek; *main dish,* woven plait of salmon & brill with a saffron and asparagus sauce; fresh selection of desserts made up daily. Wines from £5.95 to £23.00; they have two Bordeaux wines 'specially chosen for Newcastle United' – bottled in Bordeaux and embossed with their own crest.

LINDEN HALL HOTEL
Longhorsley, Northumberland.
☎0670-516611.

A beautiful, well kept country house hotel set in its own extensive grounds, about half an hour's drive from Newcastle. The building itself is grand and imposing, and the dining-room has rather a formal atmosphere. There is a varied menu with quite a lot of game and rather elaborate desserts, and the wine cellar is very well stocked. In the higher price bracket, but definitely worth driving out to, especially in the summer, to appreciate the surroundings.

21 QUEEN STREET
Queen St, Quayside, Newcastle.
☎222 0755.

A new top class restaurant opened in 1988 by Terry and Susan Laybourne. Terry, previously head chef at the Fishermans Lodge, is a caring chef who likes to pop out of the kitchen to meet diners and ask them how they liked their meal. Menus are seasonal. A typical one might feature: *starters,* cappuccino of wild mushroom soup with a frothy topping and asparagus; or, smoked salmon with salad and citrus fruits; or, Northumbrian game paté with an orange and port wine sauce; *main dish,* roast partridge, or honey roast duck breast with oriental spices; *dessert,* sticky toffee pudding with hot butterscotch sauce. *Speciality:* medallions of Kielder venison. Lunchtime menus (popular with businessmen) include a fixed price three-course meal with coffee and petit fours at £11.20. Evenings à la carte only: closed Sundays and Mondays.

WATERSIDE RESTAURANT
Quayside, Newcastle. ☎232 5537.

Asked if the Waterside is the only totally English restaurant in the city, Sandra says 'We believe it's the only one in the North East.' A set price lunch costs £3.95; dinner, £8.95 with, say, grilled sardines followed by pheasant and chestnut casserole. This is a typical English restaurant used mostly by business people; booking necessary Friday and Saturday evenings. They have 9 tables, and offer an excellent selection of dishes. Typical menu: *starter*, Stilton fritter; *main dish*, whisky fillet. *Speciality:* King Prawn Waterside. Open 12 – 2pm & 7 – 11pm (last orders); closed Mondays.

BESOM BARN
Longframlington, Morpeth.
☎066570-627.
English restaurant with a wide-ranging menu and wine list. *Speciality:* game pie. Book in advance.

THE BARN
Leazes Park Rd, Newcastle.
☎261 6373.
Trendy bistro where the tables are surrounded by antiques and bric-a-brac (which are for sale). There is live music on Tuesday and Thursday nights, which is particularly popular with students. Plenty of choice for veggies and carnivores. *Speciality:* pork with aubergines & spinach; also a three-dish special which allows you to sample several different things.

BRITANNIA BEEFEATER STEAK HOUSE
Front St, Cleadon. ☎536 4198.
This restaurant has 110 tables, with a very varied menu at reasonable prices. Promotions are run at various times throughout the year.

BLACKFRIARS BRASSERIE
Monk St, Newcastle. ☎261 5945.
Blackfriars is a 13th century Dominican friary later used by nine Craft Guilds. Now restored, it houses several craft workshops and the restaurant, which is listed in Egon Ronay's *Just a Bite*, offering English and European dishes throughout the day. *Specialities:* lamb souvlaki; deep fried ice cream. There are 30 tables and you don't have to book in advance; but it's only open during the day.

CAFÉ MOZART RESTAURANT
County Hotel, Neville St, Newcastle. ☎232 2471 x 5.
Comfortable café with first class service, often with a pianist providing music while you eat. The chef is a bright and cheerful young man, formerly of the Three Tuns, Durham. Fixed price set lunch: £7.95; carvery: from £8.50. Two course evening meal, £9.50; three course dinner, £12; four courses, £13.50. A la carte menu could include: melon & pineapple marinated in port, stir-fry crispy vegetables in a mild curry sauce on rice, or a pancake with chicken and sweetcorn with sauce Mornay, followed by grilled lamb cutlets served on a mint & redcurrant glaze or pan-fried chicken supreme filled with salmon mousse served in a rich saffron sauce. This café also launched the Restaurant Society Club in which members can dine two for the price of one at several other top restaurants. Open 12am–2pm & 6.30–10pm Mon – Fri; from 7pm weekends.

CONVIVIUM RESTAURANT
Holiday Inn, Great North Rd, Seaton Burn. ☎236 5432 x 87.
This is as inviting as its name. Spend half an hour or more in this Holiday Inn and you feel on holiday. Help yourself buffet in the centre of the restaurant...though all you need do is look a little weary and a member of staff will bring and replenish your plate. Fixed price lunch: £13.50, including bottle of wine, and dinner in the evening costs the same, but no

wine! A la carte: £9.95 – £11.95, main course; £2–£5, puddings.

ENTERTAINERS RESTAURANT
Crest Hotel, New Bridge St, Newcastle. ☎232 6191 x 639.
So called because stars of the theatre are said to dine here. They make a point of catering for all needs: meat eater, veggie, children, slimmers and diabetics (even with a run down of calories). Either help yourself or à la carte: average main course £13.25. Open 12.30 – 1.45pm & 6.30 – 10pm; late supper menu from 11pm on request.

ESLINGTON VILLA HOTEL
Station Rd, Low Fell. ☎487 6017.
Elegant country house style hotel, with own car park. Small but interesting selection of main courses, including quite a variety of vegetables, with regular changes of menu; good wine selection; higher price bracket.

FALSTAFFS
Theatre Royal, Grey St, Newcastle. ☎261 1904.
Silver service restaurant inside the theatre named after Shakespeare's famous megaglutton. The menu of French and traditional English dishes has a theatrical presentation: headed with First Act, followed by an Interval and Finale. Performances: 12–2pm & 6–10.30pm, but no show on Sundays.

FIDDLERS THREE
Albion Rd, Windy Nook. ☎469 2219.
Menu has a good selection of reasonably priced dishes. *Speciality:* Carvery roast of the day, with fresh veg and potatoes or salad bar, then dessert and and coffee/tea, all for £4.75; Sunday lunch is from £3.60.

GIBSIDE ARMS HOTEL
Front St, Whickham. ☎488 9292.
Informal restaurant used mainly by businessmen and families. Varied range of reasonably priced meals: e.g. *starter*, chicken liver paté with bramble glacé and toast; *main dish*, pan-fried trout stuffed with celery and walnuts. *Speciality:* medallions of beef. Also special lunchtime menu.

KNIGHTS RESTAURANT
Leazes Park Rd, Newcastle. ☎261 7045.
A lovely restaurant, just changing from its red, grey and wickerwork furnishing theme to an older, more layered, and older than yesterday theme. Most expensive dishes on the menu are the beef fillets, beef wellington, and beef lombardo (£9.25 each). Open: Tues – Fri. Owners Michael Phillips Knight and his wife Hazel are opening a carvery next-door.

LADY ELEANORS
Quayside, North Shields. ☎257 1525.
Best-selling novelist Carol Clewlow (of *A Woman's Guide to Adultery* and *Keeping the Faith*) started up Lady Eleanors with members of the pop group Lindisfarne, but they've now gone their separate ways. The accent though is still on the age of Rock, while curiously the rather relaxing decor is based on the kind of furniture your mother couldn't wait to throw out, like 1930s-type chairs, tables and sideboards. The building, situated right on the waterfront, is a beautiful early 19th century granary which still has its original three feet thick slab stone walls, flagstone floors and vaulted ceiling, and there are wonderful views from the balcony both upriver and down to the mouth of the Tyne.   With the fish quay just half a mile away, speciali-

ties of the house include freshly caught turbot and lemon sole. The menu is small, catering for both meat eaters (steak, chicken, stir-fried beef fillet) and veggies (fresh pasta with Lady Eleanor's own special sauce and asparagus coulibac in hollandaise sauce). Starters, £1.25 – £3; main course, £3.75 – £9; puds, £2.50, from oranges in grand marnier to delicious American ice creams and French sorbets. Special brunch on Saturdays and Sundays, with families particularly welcome: full English breakfast (with prize-winning sausages, hash browns etc), kippers, kedgeree, eggs benedict, eggs florentine. The wine list includes good value house wines (Cote du Rhone and crisp white Catherine Bergerac) as well as fine wines at the higher end of the price scale. The bistro-style atmosphere is fun and informal. Open for brunch at 11.30am, for dinner at 7pm (last orders 10pm): booking advisable Thurs, Fri and Sat (closed Mon). Highly recommended.

LE JARDIN RESTAURANT
Northumbria Hotel, Osborne Rd, Jesmond, Newcastle. ☎281 7881.
Le Jardin restaurant is a very pleasant place, busy with plants, statues and, when the occasion demands it, a Cupid. A four course meal at lunchtimes with a choice of English and French dishes costs from £6.75; dinner will cost from £11.50.

LORD CREWE ARMS
Blanchland, nr. Consett, Co. Durham. ☎043 475–251
Situated south of the Tyne, Blanchland is the flower of Northumbrian villages, and this hotel is the place to go on a summer evening for dinner, or for a lunch stop while driving round this delightful part of old Hexhamshire. The 13th century building used to be an abbey, and there are beautiful views from the restaurant over the Derwent Valley. For your starter, try the popular crab claws sautéd in garlic butter, or smoked pork with pine kernels. Main dish specialities include local pheasant with apples and calvados; Slaley Forest venison; escalope of veal paprika and mushrooms; and fillets of pork with apricots and brandy. The favourite Lord Crewe dessert is raspberry torte. There is a set price menu at £15. Bar lunches are available 12–2pm during the week, with a three-course Sunday lunch served in the restaurant, and the restaurant is open seven nights a week.

MOAT HOUSE HOTEL
Coast Rd, Newcastle. ☎262 8989
Carvery with a choice of starters and always a few extra dishes to choose from; a four course meal for £11. At dinner the price is the same: 'Well, the meal is the same,' explained a still in touch assistant. Children under 12 are served half-price meals. Open all week except Saturday lunchtimes (reserved for wedding parties).

OSCARS RESTAURANT
Royal Station Hotel, Neville St, Newcastle. ☎232 0781.
Open evenings 7 – 9.30pm (last orders) but give the chef an excuse to open at lunchtime and he most certainly will. A set price dinner costs £12.50, but go for the à la carte, with a starter of smoked salmon, and maybe that classic favourite, roast beef and Yorkshire pudding. Oscars, like its name, is very star-touched, with lovely Hollywood pictures and atmosphere.

PLAYHOUSE KITCHEN
Newcastle Playhouse, Barras Bridge. ☎261 0703.
The theatre is one of the few places you can go in town for a quiet drink mid-evening (no jukebox!), and is often half empty during an act of whatever play or pantomime is going on upstairs. However, this is not always so; bands play in the foyer up to 3 times a week (listings available in the *Evening Chronicle*). The bar-style lunch menu offers 'slightly unusual salads': orange, raisin, bean sprout and red cabbage. The menu is wholefood but not particularly vegetarian. The early evening pre-show bite includes hot meals. A typical menu offers homemade soup for the starter and curried chicken mayonnaise as the main course, followed by banana and cream flan or chocolate mud pie. The Playhouse is also one of the few places in Newcastle where you can hear live Sunday lunchtime jazz. There is a full public bar open at lunchtimes and in the evening.

TYNESIDE COFFEE ROOMS
Pilgrim St, Newcastle. ☎261 9291
A coffee shop/restaurant in the Tyneside Cinema building, a Newcastle attraction in itself. It is well established, with a relaxed atmosphere; the decor is 1930s style, including the fans which swing slowly, keeping the temperature cool. Tables are situated in a spacious and airy room with two comfortable corner areas. The customers range from students to shoppers and businessmen. The staff are friendly and the food pleasant and reasonably priced. Open 10am – 9pm Monday to Saturday.

STAGE BISTRO
Westgate Rd, Newcastle.
☎261 8217.
This theatre restaurant has a good atmosphere and you can allegedly mingle with the stars. They have a special jazz night every 2 weeks. The meals are all 'home-cooked'; bar meals and à la carte after 7.30. Typical menu: *starter*, prawn cocktail; *main courses*, fresh fish, homemade quiche, liver and onions; *dessert*, knickerbocker glory. There are 30 tables and you don't have to book in advance.

TRELLIS RESTAURANT
Stakis Airport Hotel, Wolsington, Newcastle. ☎0661–24911
The lunch menu changes every day, and a typical day offers a choice of soup, pates, fish starters and smoked mackerel paté followed by four or five main courses; e.g. trout or plaice with various sauces or in various wines. Set meal price is £7. Lunch 12 – 2pm every day except Saturday; open till 10pm for dinner.

WOODMANS ARMS
Whickham Park, Gateshead.
☎488 7656.
Informal restaurant with an excellent view over Newcastle, Gateshead and Northumberland. Advance booking necessary, particularly Saturdays. They also cater for vegetarians and serve bar meals.

Chinese

Tyneside has a great selection of Chinese restaurants. Many are concentrated in or around Stowell Street, which is behind Newcastle's big Co-op building in Newgate Street. But don't let that stop you looking further afield!

STOWELL STREET, or to give it its more romantic name of Newcastle's Chinatown, was until a decade ago a derelict, ageing part of the city. Today it thrives not only with Chinese community of up to 4000 people, 90% of whom are involved in catering of some kind, who rescued it from neglect, but with the Brits, who are fast becoming aficionados of Chinese restaurant food and the do-it-yourself kind from Chinese supermarkets.

Eleven years ago, our experience of Chinese food came mainly from the chow mein variety and the takeaways, neither of which appealed to the Chinese but were obligingly invented for the

> After a recording with the Northern Sinfonia we celebrated with a meal at the King Neptune in Stowell Street – previously unknown to me! Whilst waiting to be served a young blonde lady walked in who would not have looked out of place at the Cannes Film Festival! (Friday night is girls' night in Newcastle, I was told). Appetites whetted, we were shown to a table by a dinner-jacketed Chinese waiter – who spoke with the broadest Geordie accent heard in many a long year. He proved to be not only most amusing but very adept at choosing our meal – I never saw a menu! The meal was mainly fish – fresh from South Shields and Sunderland. The whole evening was most memorable, and I must repeat it. Wonderful Chinese food!
> ● THOMAS ALLEN,
>   OPERA SINGER

British. Then came the first Cantonese restaurants, including the Oriental Two Rooms, Gallowgate, now closed, which opened up the delights of Cantonese twelve-course banquets, the intricacies of chopsticks and the delicacies of true Chinese food. They flourished at first not only with the Chinese, who found it a relief to attend such outlets, particularly on Sundays for the sheer bliss of being able to play mah jong and generally have a good old Chinese gossip, but also with the English who decided it was too good an opportunity to miss.

Before then, of course, the takeaways and chow mein outlets needed distributors of Chinese ingredients, and these came from Liverpool, with its vast Chinese community, and from London.

In 1978 Peter Cheng and his wife Anne, both from Hong Kong, opened up the Wing Hong Supermarket in Westgate Road, a centre then spurned by the British with its association with 1000 year old eggs and other odd sounding items. Later Mr Cheng opened up a larger outlet in Stowell Street, so creating the foundation stone of Chinatown in Newcastle. Now there are around a dozen restaurants in and around Stowell Street specialising in the food of China's different regions including Canton, Mandarin and Szechuan, each with its own delicate characteristics and flavourings. Any evening, any day, is exciting in Newcastle's Chinatown, but Sundays have a special magic of their own, and should not be missed.

BLUE SKY
Pilgrim St, Newcastle. ☎232 2804
Said to be one of the few Chinese restaurants still specialising in the mouthwatering dim sum dishes, especially on Sundays, Blue Sky has a special lunch, takes all credit cards, and has a daily menu course choice of 24 dishes, including king prawn chop suey, special fried rice, chicken foo yung, plus a sweet.

CHINA COTTAGE
Stowell St, Newcastle. ☎232 0261
Previously called Mr Lau, this restaurant is run by the brothers who already run the nextdoor Mandarin, a jolly trio who have made China Cottage their Peking outlet. The Imperial Court of China was based in Peking (Beijing) and its influence on the culinary style of the area is still reflected in some of its more complicated and spectacular dishes such as the celebrated Peking Duck, said to be China's most glorious. *Chef's special:* giant king prawns in sauce. Special sea food banquets! (soup, choice of nine dishes and a sweet) or special three-course luncheon (£4.30).

RESTAURANTS

DRAGON HOUSE
Stowell St, Newcastle. ☎232 0868
Barry Yu and his English wife Beverley, in keeping with their oriental/occidental partnership, have employed both English and Chinese waiting staff, to cut out language problems for both nations. Barry used to be steward on the Newcastle/London Pullman and was encouraged by many local business people to take on this venture. On Sundays they have a special Sung Dynasty menu, with soup, starter, choice of main dish, sweet, and China tea or coffee, at £5.50. They also specialise in an extensive vegetarian menu with main dishes priced at £4.50, while there is a list of recommendations by the chef including Lon Hon Duck, steamed to a traditional monk's recipe, served in vegetable sauce. Barry trained in Hong Kong and specialises in vegetable sculpturing. The main type of food served is Chinese/Cantonese with a huge variety of dishes. A good wine selection ranging from £5.75 to £49.50. The Dragon House spare no effort to maintain their reputation of being one of the top restaurants in the country. Their renowned chef, Mr Yee, constantly surprises their clientele with his classic combination of traditional and innovative cuisine. Opening hours Mon – Sat 12 – 2pm & 6 – 11.30pm, Sun 12am – 11.30pm.

NEW EMPEROR
Bewick St, Newcastle. ☎222 0971.
One of the oldest Chinese restaurants in Newcastle, situated almost opposite the Central Station. A good place to take a party of people: try the banquet, with a seemingly unending procession of different dishes paraded before you on a revolving turntable. Open from 6pm till 4am, Monday to Saturday, and 12–2pm on Sundays.

GREAT WALL
Bath Lane, Newcastle. ☎232 0517
Vegetarians particularly like this restaurant because they have a special veggie menu and set veggie dinners for two or four people at £9 a head. Monday to Friday they have special buffets of all kinds, 7.30 – 10.30pm, from £7.80 to £8.80 and three course lunch Monday to Saturday costs £3.30. The cuisine is Cantonese, with seafood a speciality.

HAPPINESS INN
Percy St, Newcastle. ☎232 5969
Open seven days a week, this restaurant is run by Tony Chen, who has the distinction of being one of the longest serving and perhaps the tallest Chinese restaurant owner in Newcastle! At weekends he has launched a series of Chinese buffets because he recognises that not every English person knows (even after all this time) what to order. This way customers can pick, choose and experiment. Tony offers a variety of dishes such as chicken and sweetcorn soup, or fruit juice, a twelve-course choice of main meals including yung chow fried rice, char siu pork and mushrooms with boiled rice as well as a range of English dishes. Open: 11.30am – 11.30pm, seven days a week.

JADE GARDEN
Stowell St, Newcastle. ☎261 5889
Believed to be the first Chinese restaurant in Stowell Street, with a nice greenish decor, the Jade Garden offers a range of set dinners for two; six dishes will set you back £18, while the same for 14 people will cost £126. They also offer an extensive à la carte menu and take all kinds of credit cards. The Jade Garden has been recommended every year for the past five years by the *Good Food Guide.*

KING NEPTUNE
Stowell St, Newcastle. ☎261 6657
A comfortable, smart Chinese restaurant which tends to get very busy, particularly on a Saturday night, so booking is essential. The bar area gets very cramped as there are only very few seats. However, like most Chinese restaurants, it is extremely efficiently run and the service is excellent as is the food. Crispy aromatic duck with pancakes can always be recommended. The food and service are so consistently good. The King Neptune is the natural dining place of top Chinese cookery expert and author Ken Hom, when he is in the area. Possibly the most expensive Chinese restaurant (they whip away the ashtrays to clean them almost before you flick your ash!), their Sunday lunch, four dishes and rice plus tea or coffee, costs £8.50. They hold set dinners for various numbers but also offer the King Neptune Diamond menu: for two, £36; for six, £108. Also a vegetarian menu of 10 dishes.

MANDARIN
Stowell St, Newcastle. ☎261 7881
Cantonese restaurant open 12 – 2pm and 6 – 11.30pm, seven days a week. The chef's special is giant king prawns in satay sauce or chilli and salt, or boiled with special soy sauce. They also do king prawns Szechuan style, chicken satay, and fillet of beef in satay sauce.

MING DYNASTY
Stowell St, Newcastle. ☎261 5787
This is a medium-priced Chinese restaurant specialising in food from the Szechuan province of China, which is slightly hotter and spicier than other Chinese food. The restaurant is beautifully decorated in blue, gold and black, with bamboo-patterned walls and lots of plants. The dining room is large with a comfortable bar area and the food is delicious and attractively presented with very good service. One house speciality is king prawn and squid, with many other king prawn dishes, fried or sautéed, for around £8. They serve authentic barbecued Peking Duck for £25, but you must order in advance as this is one of those Chinese dishes which needs plenty of preparation. Their oysters are pan fried or fried in batter, and they have a dessert menu which is particularly extensive for the Chinese, who don't go much for puds. These include bananas, apple and pineapple fired or flambé. Set dinners range from £27 for two to £108 for eight.

ORIENTAL STAR
Cross St, Newcastle. ☎261 4511
A relaxed kind of place, which has a special lunch at £3.20. Starters are soup or fruit juice; main course, a choice from 27, including sweet and sour, chow mein, curries, chop sucy, fried rice and English dishes. This restaurant also displays a diploma called The Roll of Honour which is

awarded to master chefs, and, for more adventurous diners, will serve stewed fish head with pork and mushrooms.

PALACE GARDEN
Stowell St, Newcastle. ☎232 3117
Peter and Anne Cheng (pronounce it *Jeng*) made such a success of the Wing Hong Supermarket in Stowell Street that it seemed natural progression to open a restaurant above it – called the Palace Garden – and possibly the most ornate Chinese restaurant in the area with its emphasis on miniature willow pattern bridges over sparkling streams, filled with real fish. Try their dim sums, tiny steamed pancakes filled with a variety of sweet and savoury mixtures such as pork and prawn; crispy stuffed mixed meat, lotus paste, and sesame balls; barbecued pork cheun fun and shark's fin and Chinese mushrooms (at £1.50 per dish)...They have their own dim sum menu written in English, something unheard of for this particular dish before: they're a bit like the Spanish tapas, eaten either as starters or a full meal, and some are available during the week, but on Sundays – when the Chinese community dines out – many different kinds are wheeled around on heated trolleys and offered by waiters just as they are in Hong Kong. Open all day, every day of the week, with an á la carte menu and a grand buffet every Monday evening, 7.30–10pm, for £8.50. There is also a range of Malaysian dishes.

ROYAL CIRCLE
Stowell St, Newcastle. ☎261 2300
One of Newcastle's newest restaurants, the Royal Circle specialises in seafood. Owners Sue and Peter Lok previously ran a Chinese restaurant in Manchester, and chef Edward Au trained in Hong Kong: their Cantonese and Peking menu includes such dishes as stuffed and spicey Lover's Prawns (starter), quick fried lobster and scallops, deep fried crab claws with prawn meat and broccoli in black bean sauce, and sliced Peking duck with seasonal fruits in Peking plum sauce. The waitresses are dressed in traditional costume, and the decor is straight out of Hong Kong.

SHANGRI-LA
Stowell St, Newcastle. ☎261 2289
Shangri-La means 'earthly paradise', and this restaurant certainly has a luxurious look – more French in style than Chinese. Owner Johnny Liu wanted to create a restaurant which didn't look like all the others in Chinatown, and the same original approach informs the menu, which is Cantonese, but also has speciality vegetarian and Peking dishes and a selection not available elsewhere in the city. The chef was Hong Kong trained, and previously worked for several years in other Newcastle restaurants. Johnny's brother Eddie Liu is the restaurant manager.

Curry

Tyneside may not have as many Indian restaurants as it has Chinese, but the range is superb – from the rock bottom prices of the students' favourite, Eastern Taste, to the exquisite Sachins. Or go to South Shields and try one of the many curryhouses on Ocean Road...

DARAZ TANDOORI
Holly Ave West, Jesmond, Newcastle. ☎281 8431
A traditional Indian restaurant with tables set in alcoves but rather a small bar area. The usual sort of menu, but with a few different, very tasty specialities and all cooked to a high standard. Unfortunately you do often have to wait quite a long time for your meal, but as they cook everything fresh, this has to be accepted and it is certainly very good when it arrives. Average price range for an Indian restaurant with easy parking but not the place to go if you want a quick meal.

EASTERN TASTE
Stanhope St, Fenham, Newcastle. ☎273 9406
A very friendly Indian takeaway and eat-in with a traditional menu with a home-made feel to it: wonderful food and cheap. The prices are rock bottom, so it's much used by students: a decent-sized curry, rice and usual extras can come to as little as £3.50! It has very much an Indian café-style atmosphere: the decor isn't up to much, but the place is friendly and bustling. Take your own booze: or it's a choice of Coca Cola or water. Be prepared for a long wait, unless you ring in beforehand. An ideal venue for a cheap, fun night out.

GOLDEN BENGAL
Groat Market, Newcastle.
☎232 4035
One of several Indian restaurants in the Bigg Market area, the Golden Bengal is well-known for its friendly and helpful waiters. Popular at the weekends, it's just the place to tuck into a vindaloo after closing time. We spotted actor Timothy West here, when he was appearing in a play at the Theatre Royal, who was quickly adopted by a bunch of revellers.

KOH-I-NOOR
Cloth Market, Newcastle.
☎232 5379
Good tandoori restaurant with a reliable, reasonably-priced menu. Two ranks of tables stretch down a dimly lit cavern-like room sometimes virtually empty at lunchtimes (despite an excellent lunch menu) and early evening but full to bursting later in the evenings. The chicken tikka marsala in its delicious red creamy sauce is the best we've tasted anywhere in Newcastle, and all the sag (spinach) dishes are good. They are also perfectionists when it comes to nan bread: the peshwari nan, with nuts and raisins, couldn't be bettered.

MAKHANI
Clayton St West, Newcastle.
☎261 0912
This is a spacious, tastefully decorated Indian restaurant with a comfortable lounge/bar area with plenty of seating. The menu contains dishes from the Punjab area of India which are unusual and delicious and can be quite rich. Particularly notable are the enormous fruit and nut filled nans and the tandoori starters which arrive on a hot skillet. The staff are friendly and very helpful and the service is good. It is, however, slightly more expensive than the usual run of the mill Indian restaurant, but well worth it.

MOTI JHEEL
Waterloo Street, Newcastle.
☎232 7952
Tucked away behind Marlborough Crescent, almost opposite Rockshots, the Moti Jheel is not to be confused with the nearby Moti Mahal: the food is just as good, but a little cheaper in price. The Moti Jheel was one of the first tandoori restaurants in Newcastle, remembered by many for the fishpond and fountain in the bar (recently removed). However, it still has its moving waterfall picture on the wall, and manages to combine unbelievable bad taste in the decor (so overpowering that it's really quite magnificent!) with impeccable good taste in the food. The courteous waiters will sit the ladies with their backs to the walls, giving them a good view of the curious wooden canopies and panels embellished with hundreds of artificial flowers, while the men can view erotic pictures above the heads of their female companions. The menu includes a reliable selection of curries and biriani dishes, but if you want something really good, choose one of the tandoori specialities (like the Moti Jheel Special) or the karaya, pasanda and jalfrezi specialities. Skip the starters and have several side dishes with the main meal, like the excellent (spicy!) Bombay potato or the sag aloo; the vegetable pilaw is almost a meal in itself. Or, for a veritable feast, try the thali or the non-vegetable thali, both of which give you several pots of interesting curries plus raitha and nan bread.

MOTI MAHAL
Forth Place, Newcastle. ☎232 9148
Near the station, just behind Clayton Street West, this is the place for genuine Indian cuisine: and they do not subscribe to the curry and chips mentality! The Moti Mahal was the first genuine Tandoori restaurant in the North East, and their original clay ovens were imported from India. The most popular meal on their menu is chicken tikka massala. They also offer an excellent four-course executive lunch for £3.50.

NEW BENGAL
Ridley Place, Newcastle.
☎232 5945
Situated just off the top of Northumberland Street (handy for the City Hall), this is one of the few restaurants in that part of the city centre. It's a middle-of-the-road, reliable place to go for a curry where the food is always tasty and the prices aren't excessive. If you don't know your way round the menu, we'd recommend one of the four set menus, which are all very reasonable.

RUCHI
Royal Court, Bigg Market, Newcastle. ☎232 0159
The Ruchi is an excellent Punjabi restaurant sometimes overlooked because it's hidden away down one of the courts leading off the Bigg

Market (just down from Brahms & Liszt). Don't be put off by the bare stairwell leading up to the restaurant, or the spartan decor of the place itself: it's well worth a visit: the menu may look familiar, but you'll find each of your usual favourites comes out hotter and spicier with Ruchi's special Punjabi recipes. Keep a pint of lager handy for when you bite on a hidden chilli in the sauce!

RUPALI
Bigg Market, Newcastle.
☎232 8629
An Indian restaurant with a difference. Mr Latif and his staff are friendly and professional, and certainly know how to market themselves. The comprehensive menu is well written, giving you a real taste of what is to come, with a description of the background to each dish. In a colour brochure, Mr Latif details the '16 Reasons why you should dine at the Rupali'. These include low price lunchtime specials, happy nights on Thursdays (when a three-course meal with liqueur coffee and a glass of wine is only £6.95), a 10% student discount and, of course, an excellent range of freshly cooked dishes. And, believe it or not, although it's been recommended every year for the past five years by the *Good Food Guide*, the Rupali is not all that expensive, but don't tell anyone!

SACHINS
Forth Banks, Newcastle.
☎261 9035
One of the best places to eat in Newcastle, situated behind the Central Station. Sachins is an up-market Punjabi restaurant: where you go for a special occasion when you're prepared to pay extra for something really exquisite, or when someone else is paying. Mr Rawlley has run Sachins from when it opened in 1983, and has now taken over. Ask what the trifle of gold lying on top of one of your dishes is, and the answer will come 'Gold Leaf'. Later on he will tell you how many carats. The most popular meal is a set meal for two for £26.00. All the dishes on the menu are cooked separately without any base curry giving the food its own flavour and particular taste. It's a good place to take hard-to-please southerners, especially the ones who go on and on about how London restaurants are so good that they *really* couldn't live anywhere else: at Sachins they'll have to eat their words. Make sure you book first. Opening times: 12am – 2pm & 6 – 11.15pm.

A TASTE OF INDIA
High St, Gosforth. ☎285 0525
This new, friendly Indian restaurant is in Gosforth's Old Assembly Rooms, and specialises in tandoori, korma and vegetarian dishes. It has the biggest party and function room in the Gosforth/Jesmond area, but is also just the place for an intimate dinner for two. This is the management's third restaurant: their others are in Prudhoe and Keswick. Open seven days a week: 12.30–2.30pm & 6–11.30pm; special Sunday buffet 12–2pm.

Ocean Road, South Shields

A four-course meal for under a fiver!

South Shields could easily claim to be the curry capital of the North East. Ocean Road, five minutes' walk from South Shields Metro station, boasts nine Indian restaurants (and one Chinese) within 200 yards. They may not all be top class in style, but they certainly give value for money, with most offering four-course meals with free wine on Tuesdays and Sundays for under £5! You can find them open until at least 2am to cater for revellers from the nearby nightclubs.

Welcome to Paradise

PARADISE TANDOORI
86 Ocean Road. ☎456 6098
This is the first restaurant you arrive at on Ocean Road coming from the town. It is rather small and the glittery wallpaper is held together in places by sellotape. But all of the usual Indian dishes are available and are tasty and well presented.

NASEEB TANDOORI
88 Ocean Road. ☎456 4294
Owned by the friendly Mr Choudhury, a Bangladeshi who has been proprietor for the past ten years, the Naseeb offers the usual Indian menu. It is very busy at weekends, Tandoori dishes being the most popular. A four-course meal is available on Tuesdays and Sundays for £4.75 with free wine!

MOMOTAJ TANDOORI
144 Ocean Road. ☎455 5130
The Momotaj serves good quality dishes – especially to late night revellers. Perhaps not the best choice of a romantic outing, but the low prices make it attractive.

JOY KING
118 Ocean Road. ☎427 1577
The only Chinese restaurant on Ocean Road. Opened in November 1988, it has already taken off, so much so that it is necessary to book every night since there are only 11 tables at the moment. The chef Mr Chung previously worked in a popular Stowell Street restaurant and therefore all the usual Peking cuisine is available at much cheaper prices. The special set dinners are the best value for money. An interesting range of oriental wines are available.

TANDOORI INTERNATIONALE
97 Ocean Road. ☎456 2000
A slightly more expensive restaurant which also serves a good selection of English meals, this is Ocean Road at its most up-market. The decor is quite plush and English music is piped in the background. The Sunday night special is a must at £4.95.

DID YOU KNOW that South Shields, in common with many other British seaports, such as Cardiff and Liverpool, long ago came to terms with the assimilation of an ethnic minority? – a situation reflected in the large number of long established restaurants specialising in Indian food!

Long before today's numerous Indian restaurants had opened in Newcastle – and even in London – the advent of the steamship in the middle of the last century led to the widespread employment of Indians, hailing mainly from East India, who were known as the lascars. They were stokers aboard the British vessels and eventually settled in the ports from which their ships sailed.

Among these ports was our own South Shields, and along the whole stretch of Ocean Road the evidence of their integration can be found. In fact, as long ago as the 1950s (and some say before!), the folk of South Shields were as familiar with Korma, Tandoori and other regional dishes of India, as most of us are now. ●

SHANTI TANDOORI
150 Ocean Road. ☎455 7014
A smart restaurant with a few secluded alcoves for those wanting privacy. This one is recommended for a romantic evening and the chance to find out if all those hot spices really do have aphrodisiac qualities.

STAR OF INDIA
194 Ocean Road. ☎456 2210
The most popular on Ocean Road. Established in 1960, it was the first ever Indian restaurant in the area. The special buffet with three courses for £3.95 and is highly recommended. It is best to book at weekends.

INDIA BRASSERIE
146 Ocean Road. ☎456 8800
A spacious and comfortable restaurant with a small fish pond in the bar area. The special price meal is incredibly cheap at only £4.50 for four courses.

OMARS
216 Ocean Road. ☎454 2835
A very modern establishment with Austrian blinds adorning the windows and hanging floral arrangements in the lower level bar area. The only restaurant to offer a free taxi on Mondays and Wednesdays to the restaurant and home again if you are in a party of four or more and you live within a five mile radius. The English owners, Mr and Mrs Pippet, own the local taxi firm too. On Thursdays and Sundays if you buy one drink you get one free.

DILSHAD
224 Ocean Road. ☎455 3094
The Bangladeshi owner and chef of this establishment is Mozzomil Ali, who has worked there for the past 28 years and his experience is reflected in the general quality of the food.

Italian

It seems incredible to imagine now, with Newcastle resembling Rimini or Lido de Jessolo with its abundance of Italian eating places, but 25 years ago few Geordies knew what pizza or pasta were!

Then the Italian invasion began – but it was by no means plain sailing for the early Italian pioneers who came here intent on making their fortunes. At first most worked as waiters in English hotels and restaurants. Several of them then got together and decided to open their own restaurant on Tyneside.

The first was the Ristorante Italia in Low Fell, run by Pasquale Fulgenzi, Mario Neri and Dante Calzini. In 1965 Pasquale and Mario moved across the river and opened Newcastle's first Italian restaurant, Ristorante Roma in Collingwood Street. But they weren't prepared for the English suspicion when it came to their food!

'All they wanted was steak, chips, prawn cocktails and Black Forest Gateaux,' recalled Pasquale, who runs the restaurant today. 'They wouldn't even try our Italian food.' So they cooked up a steaming plate of spaghetti, served it with bolognaise, and the staff tucked into it. Slowly the mingled odours of meat, garlic and tomato, wafted across the restaurant and the Geordies, for once, took their eyes off their steak-filled plates and gazed across.

'We offered them samples,' said Pasquale. 'They tried it, liked it, and next time came in and ordered that as well as many other Italian dishes.' The Brits were hooked and the restaurant has thrived ever since.

The extraordinary growth of Newcastle's Italian eating scene began there, with Mario Neri going off to open his own Ristorante Mario in Westgate Road, while Dante Calzini has set up several Tyneside restaurants, most recently Dante's (Il Cappuccino) in Nelson Street.

AMIGOS
Mosley St, Newcastle. ☎232 1111
Don't be put off by the fact that Amigos is to be found inside one of the scruffiest and most neglected buildings in the city centre. Amigos is quite smart inside, even with its rather garish pink neon strip-lighting. At £2.95 for a pizza or pasta, a meal here is not going to break the bank.

CAPRICCIO
Groat Market, Newcastle.
☎232 1599
One of Newcastle's most popular

pizzerias, Capriccio's is always packed when the Bigg Market outside is at its most lively. Owner Sergio Deltodesco has worked in the restaurant business for over 20 years – throughout the world, but mostly in Switzerland – while his head waiter Luigi is a Venetian with 'the charm of our Italian gondoliers'. Franco the chef says his most popular dishes are lasagne (£2.30), Chicken Kiev (£4) and Steak Diane (£5). His antipasto (£1.85) is almost a meal in itself, but an excellent starter when shared between two. The lunchtime menu offers any pizza or pasta for £1.80, and a carafe of rather good Merlot house red is only £4.30.

CASA NOSTRA
Dean St, Newcastle. ☎261 7026
Hidden away above Prontapizza (you have to walk through the takeaway to get to it), the Trattoria Casa Nostra is one of Tyneside's little-known culinary gems. As this guide went to press it was being refurbished, and due to reopen in September 1989. It has to be emphasised that the restaurant is entirely separate from the takeaway below. In the kitchen above they have their own pasta machine: you'll really notice the difference between their fresh pasta and the pasta served in some restaurants if you try their spaghetti, cannelloni, tagliatelli or lasagna al forno (which is particularly good). Their pasta is so good that it seems almost a crime to choose the pizza sometimes, but the pizzas are almost the equal of the pasta – always piping hot, deliciously doughy, and stuffed with the freshest of fresh tasting ingredients. The service is jolly, the prices are very reasonable, and the lunch menu is a snip. The house wine is cheap in price but first-rate in quality, and comes in an earthenware jug which seems to replenish many more glasses than it would appear capable of filling. The soups are also very good, and there are some excellent desserts, including some incredibly naughty (but nice) gateaux, with generous portions. The Death by Chocolate is a killer: layers of chocolate, chocolate gateau, chocolate cream and chocolate mousse! On your way out, you can buy pasta to take home from Prontapizza downstairs, as well as a range of other Italian delicacies.

COLOMBO
Pudding Chare, Newcastle.
☎261 9955
There are two good pizzerias opposite one another on Pudding Chare, just off the Bigg Market, Mamma Mia, which is generally reckoned to do the better pizzas, and Pizzeria Colombo, where the fresh pasta is really good. Colombo's is an oasis of calm: the curtains and carpet muffle the sound of the Bigg Market outside, so that you're really quite surprised when you leave and are suddenly assailed by all the noise.

DANTE'S
Nelson St, Newcastle. ☎261 7502
Dante Calzini is one of Tyneside's Italian food pioneers. His latest move, after Dante & Piero, was to take over Il Cappuccino Pizzeria – now Dante's. As well as having a regular menu including such specialities as Tris della Casa (three different flavours of pasta) and Risotto alla Contadina (ham, chicken, peas, tomato, wine), Dante now puts on a weekly special menu, ranging from (when we went there) omelette chasseur, and liver and onions – both £2.20 – to Dover sole at £7.20. Open: Mon–Sat, 11.30am–2.30pm & 5.30–11pm.

DANTE & PIERO
Neville St, Newcastle. ☎232 4035
Opposite Central Station, this is a very large restaurant with its own pub-style bar area and disco: it fills all the rooms originally built for the Geordie Pride pub, which it replaced. The pizzas and pastas are as good as you'll find in most places in the city centre, but the creamy, chocolatey continental trifle is an absolute must. It's usually quite noisy, and is a good place to go with a lively gang of people. It's not unusual to see hen-night tables of girls shrieking at singing telegram Tarzans in loin cloths, or a French chambermaid oo-lah-lahing a bunch of lads out on a birthday night razz.

DA VINCI'S
Osborne Rd, Jesmond, Newcastle.
☎281 5284
This is one of the most up-market pizza restaurants in Newcastle. It is most popular with yuppies, business people, nearby hotel guests and people who want to eat somewhere a little special. However, the recently introduced Happy Hour from 6 to 7pm has brought pizza and pasta prices down to £2 each, and has widened the market to students and others in the early evening. The menu has many other choices apart from the usual ones, with the veal is a chef's speciality, as are the garlic potato skins for starters. The portions are generous. The atmosphere is pleasant and the decor quite plush with drapes and chandeliers. Service is particularly charming! Book beforehand if you want to dine after 8pm, particularly at weekends. If you leave it too late the sweet trolley becomes gradually less spectacular!

DON VITOS
Pilgrim St, Newcastle. ☎232 8923
This restaurant is very reasonably priced. The lunch menu is £2.25 for three courses including the main course of the day, which is often something like fresh mussels. The portions are large and fresh Tuscan bread is delivered twice daily and placed on the table for free. The evening menu is excellent. Try having a half portion of pasta as a starter, and then splash out on a beautifully cooked steak au poivre, steak in a wine and mushroom sauce, or pollo valdostano (chicken with cheese and tomato encased in breadcrumbs). The pizzas and veal dishes are also delicious. It also has a slightly cheaper takeaway food menu.

FRANCESCA'S
Manor House Rd, Jesmond, Newcastle. ☎281 6586
This extremely popular restaurant in trendy, residential Jesmond is well known for its cheap good food and house wine, friendly informal service, but mostly for its long queues and minutes waiting to get a seat. It is impossible to book in advance and closes quite early in the evening so there is a mad rush in the early evenings. Fairly basic and cramped inside, but with its own unique atmosphere and charm, families and young children are made to feel very welcome here and are fussed over by the waiters who are all extremely efficient and pleasant. The pizza and chips combination is a favourite among children and adults alike, and it is mostly families and students who find the atmosphere so appealing and become regulars more often than not. You can eat very cheaply; from £5 – £7 per head, and you can have a substantial meal here for two for around £15 including wine. Half portions are available for children or for starters. Their pizzas have thin bases and lots of topping like traditional Italian home cooking. The

pizzas and garlic bread are particularly good. The only drawbacks are 9pm closing, parking problems and, as you can't book tables, you always have to queue if you arrive after about 6pm.

ITALIA RISTORANTE
Durham Rd, Low Fell. ☎487 9362
The Italia was the first Italian restaurant on Tyneside. Unpretentious and friendly, it doesn't serve pizzas but has plenty of other well-cooked Italian dishes at reasonable prices. Don't be put off by the uninviting exterior. From a wide selection of starters, the Parma ham and melon is as good as you'll find anywhere. Main courses include all the usual pasta dishes, a good choice of fish – try the Trotta alla griglia (two *large* grilled trout), chicken, and the chef's speciality – beef dishes. These include mouthwatering tender steaks in imaginative sauces. The house wine, however, is rather disappointing, so choose from the wine list instead.

ITALIAN JOB
Dean St, Newcastle. ☎261 4371
There's a cosy and relaxed atmosphere at the Italian Job, with tables on different levels and checked tablecloths. The restaurant was decked out as *Weegees* in *Stormy Monday*, the recent Sting film with a Tyneside setting. They don't open at lunchtime, but there's a special price of £2 for pizza and pasta, 5.30 – 7.30pm. Children are welcome, with a £1.75 menu for under-12s, and a magician from 6.30 to 7.30pm every Saturday.

L'ARAGOSTA
Grey St, Newcastle. ☎232 4142
Good quality, middle price range, traditional Italian restaurant, which does particularly good fish dishes. Expect to pay between £15 and £21 per head. How about this for a starter?...oysters in haddock, £3.95; then, as main course, a nice big portion of veal for £6.95. Open Monday to Friday for lunch and dinner, and Saturday dinner only; closed on Sundays.

LA STALLA
Pilgrim St, Newcastle. ☎232 4220
If you're looking for a friendly Italian restaurant offering a good choice of dishes for a very reasonable price, then La Stalla is the place to go: before 7pm and all night on Wednesdays pizzas or pasta are only £1.75, one of the cheapest of Newcastle's many early evening specials. Popular with young people and students, there's also a dance floor. The atmosphere is cosy in both of La Stalla's two large rooms, with candles on the tables, and good service. Particularly recommended is the rigatoni al forno – pasta and rich bolognese sauce with melted cheese on the top, hot from the oven.

LA TOSCANA
Leazes Pk Rd, Newcastle.
☎232 5871
Good quality, middle price range, traditional Italian restaurant. All of chef Keith Ward's meals are luscious and lovely, but to take one special example, here's a meal that was put on for a 16th birthday celebration recently: the starter course was melon with ham and then a very attractive cannelloni; then a luscious consommé; then we were ordered to have a rest. The main course was arrosto misto – just as exciting as it sounds – three types of roast meat accompanied by interesting vegetables and salads. Rest number two was followed by fruit salad, another sort of pudding (all very Italian!) and then coffee and cream and lovely liqueur. The price for this particular meal was £12.75 a head. Open:

12–2pm Mon–Fri; dinner, 7–11pm, Mon–Sat.

MAMMA MIA
Pudding Chare, Newcastle.
☎232 7193
Hidden away in Pudding Chare just off the Bigg Market is another good value Italian pasta-and-pizzeria, small and candle-lit and famous for its massive square pizzas hanging over the edges of your plate. Try Mamma Mia's own pizza, which has everything you can think of on top. But watch out for the waiters, girls – they're a red-blooded lot!

MARCO POLO
Dean St, Newcastle. ☎232 5533
Situated in the lovely Cathedral Buildings on Dean Street, Marco Polo is run by a friendly Italian family team who give customers a warm welcome. Always packed, the atmosphere is cosy and intimate, especially after the pubs have closed. They have the usual range of pizzas and pasta, but they're all very tasty.

MARIO
Westgate Rd, Newcastle.
☎232 0708
Mario Neri has been involved in running Italian restaurants on Tyneside since the sixties. He runs the top-class Ristorante Mario alongside his Pizzeria La Dolce Vita, so you can go for a quick pizza or pasta, or treat yourself to a beautiful fish dish or one of the house speciality steaks. He serves 12 different kinds of steak, from Bistecca Napoletana (with cheese and asparagus – £6.55) to a £9 T-bone; and 12 different veal dishes, all for just over £5. A three-course lunch with coffee costs £5.95, with main courses including several of Mario's delicious fish, veal and steak dishes.

PORTOFINO
Pilgrim St, Newcastle. ☎261 7276
Portofino has the feel of a traditional Italian pizza café, and has an exceptional range of menus, Happy Hours and special offers. The quality is good, service very friendly, and it is open all day from lunchtime onwards. At the time of writing, the Happy Hour was more like a Happy Day – 12 noon till 7pm! – with all pizzas and pastas at £1.95. The lunchtime menu is particularly notable: a three-course meal with minestrone or mushrooms and garlic in white wine as the starter, followed by a choice of main course like grilled trout or chicken, and apple crumble for dessert – all for £2.95.

REEDS
St Mary's Place East, Newcastle.
☎261 5084
Formerly Joe Rigatoni's, and before that a garage, Reeds Bar & Bistro is a pizza, steak and burger joint almost opposite the Civic Centre, next to Luckies, handy for a quick bite before a City Hall concert. Don't miss the roast dinner on Sunday lunchtimes. Open: Mon–Sat 12–2.30pm & 5.30–11.30pm.

RIO'S
Bigg Market, Newcastle.
☎222 0035
Pizzeria with changing specialities posted on the blackboard, and a regular menu with pizzas, pasta, steaks and several chicken dishes. Starters include some interesting fish dishes such as bisque soup, squid and mussels. The pasta dishes are particularly good.

RISTORANTE ROMA
Collingwood St, Newcastle.
☎232 0612
This was the first Italian restaurant in Newcastle when it opened in 1965. It is very well established, with a romantic atmosphere, moderate prices, good service, and there is also a small dancing area in the lower cocktail bar which is licensed till 1am. Specialities include Veal Chop Lollobrigida (£8.85), Steak Sophia Loren (£7.95), Chicken Pascale (£7.35) and fresh ravioli (£3.85). Also popular are gamberoni, Steak Rossana and the famous Italian dessert zabaglione (egg yolk whipped in sugar and Marsala wine). They also have special gourmet evenings held on the last Sunday in every month. This is an opportunity to try different Italian dishes not known locally. The Roma is a good place for party bookings, and owner Pascale Fulgenzi is renowned for his hospitality and helpfulness; he and his waiters have been known to throw in a traditional Italian musical floorshow (with audience participation) on more than one occasion!

SANTANA
Jesmond Rd, Newcastle.
☎281 7849
The first thing you notice about Santanas is the delicious smell of garlic wafting down Jesmond Road. The second thing is the queue outside the door. This small but very cosy pizzeria is always packed — with businessmen, locals, students and families alike — and while there's often a queue you can book a table beforehand. The decor is somewhat over-the-top, with heavy wallpaper, pictures and even fairy lights, but the atmosphere is lively and intimate and reminiscent of the other Jesmond pizzeria, Francesca's (their prices are similar too). The prawns in garlic and the pastas are particularly good, and there's a special price of £2.10 for pizzas and pastas at lunchtimes. There are complimentary breadsticks on the tables, and they also serve children's size pizzas. Pizzeria Santana is also open on Sunday lunchtimes and from 6pm on Sunday nights. Parking is awkward as it is situated on the busy main road (at the junction of Sandyford Road and Jesmond Road).

TARLARINI'S
Leazes Pk Rd, Newcastle.
☎261 8927
Before joining Pietro Tarlarini, chef David Fletcher was head chef at the Swallow Hotel. He creates his own dishes, giving Tarlarini's Trattoria a menu which is both original and unusual. One of his starters is strawberry and melon cup (laced with drambuie and topped with dill). Each visit to Tarlarini's is likely to yield something different: David's seasonal specialities are chalked up on the blackboard, and changed almost daily. Lobsters and sea bass are among his popular dishes, and game when in season — and he makes sure the game is fresh by shooting it himself. There's also a lunchtime menu, with pasta and pizza at £2.

> When I eat in town I like to go to Tarlarini's Trattoria on Leazes Park Road. The food is delicious and quite different from other Italian restaurants. It's very friendly. There's a Scottish waiter, Ian, who always teases me about what I eat!
> ● WENDY GIBSON, TV JOURNALIST (LOOK NORTH)

FETCHAPIZZA!

Many of the above restaurants have takeaway menus, and there are in addition many pizzerias and fast food pizza places on Tyneside where you can pick up a pizza without much of a wait or by phoning first. There are also several pizza joints which offer a home delivery service – ideal for an impromptu party or for when you're just feeling lazy. They aim to deliver piping hot pizzas to your door within half an hour of getting your call. Most offer a free delivery service for orders of £5/£6 or over, but charge about 75p on orders costing less than that. However, you can easily wipe out the delivery charge by pushing your order up to the minimum price for free delivery by having a really big pizza or by having extras like garlic bread or desserts. **Prontapizza** operate a takeaway service from four different places: Dean Street, Newcastle (☎261 7026), High Street, Gosforth (☎213 0220), Kingsway, Team Valley (☎487 6003), and Station Road in Whitley Bay (☎251 4664).

Pizzaporter operate a rival service from Heaton Road, Heaton (☎276 5277), High Street, Wrekenton (☎491 0395), and Fawdon Park Road, next to Fawdon metro station (☎284 6644).

Vegetarian

CAFÉ PROCOPE
Side, Newcastle. ☎232 3848
Before she opened Café Procope, Karen Louise Kennedy had travelled extensively and worked abroad. Her staff are all young and female, with similar much travelled backgrounds, and both Caroline Hannam at the tables and chef Angela Deutschman in the kitchen help create the Café Procope's relaxed continental atmosphere. The menu specialises in French, German and Caribbean dishes: e.g. falafels and hummus; spiced red mullet in tamarind with coconut; dark Greek chocolate cake. The offbeat menu changes every three months, and includes imported bottled beers, such as Trappist monk beers brewed in Belgium, Frambozen (dark beer brewed with raspberries) and Ovval (fermenting strong beer), and they exhibit work by good local artists on the walls. The main courses are priced from £3 to £7.95 but they also encourage you to have a few starters instead, or some of the hot filled croissants, which are nearly all under £2. Much of the food is vegetarian, with at least two vegan dishes a day. The most popular meals are mushroom & broccoli goulash and chicken smoutina, which is a Greek dish (chicken cooked in a lemon and sour cream sauce). Café Procope is popular with families on Sundays, when it's open until 5pm; booking is advisable, particularly on Thursday, Friday and Saturday.

DANCE CITY
Peel Lane, Newcastle. ☎261 9820
This vegetarian café is the place to fill up after a work-out at Dance City. Also open to the public, it does takeaways as well. The home-made wholefood menu includes vegan dishes among a range of salads, pizzas, baked potatoes, etc; also home-made cakes and pastries. Omnivores welcome, but smokers have to do it outside. Open: Mon-Fri 10am–7pm (Tues & Thurs till 9pm), Sat 9am–4pm.

HARVEST KITCHEN
Pudding Chare, Newcastle.
☎232 1961
Tucked away off the Bigg Market, the Harvest Kitchen has a Japanese-influenced menu based on organic food, offering vegetarian and vegan meals, and also has a Natural Therapy Centre with information on diet, macrobiotics, etc. Open: Mon–Sat 9am–4pm.

RED HERRING
Studley Tce, Fenham, Newcastle.
☎272 3484
Vegetarian and vegan café with a small wholefood shop run by a workers co-operative. The café is friendly and simply decorated, serving good coffee, teas and fruit juices, delicious wholemeal croissants and pain chocolat as well as snacks and

RESTAURANTS

meals including Hungarian Borek, Indonesian Tempeh (soya) kebabs with pilau rice, and various Latin American dishes such as Burritos, Empanadas (pasties), and Papas à la Huancaina (potatoes filled with chilli and peanut butter sauce). The desserts are all home-made, including fruit flans, almond and cherry slices, and banana and walnut cake. Any flour used in the dishes is organic, and it's possible to have a three-course meal and coffee for £4. Open: Tues–Sat, 10am–10pm; Sun, 11am–8pm. The wholefood shop is open from 10am to 7pm, and sells the usual nuts, pulses, soya products, cheese and yoghourt, as well as clover cleaning products and Red Herring's own home-baked breads, croissants, quiches, pizzas, pasties and home-baked desserts.

SUPER NATURAL
Princess Sq, Newcastle. ☎261 2730
Newcastle's first vegetarian restaurant didn't want to be in this guide. Apparently they don't want you to know that they serve a wide range of vegetarian and vegan dishes, nor that their salads are huge and take hours to eat. They're probably open from 9.30am and you'd be likely to find them closed after 10.30pm. We think they may be closed on Sundays too. Unless it's another myth, we think you'll find the Super Natural is one of the cheapest places in Newcastle to go for a filling, healthy meal. If we'd been able to write about it, we would have recommended the broccoli in cheese and tomato sauce, and we might have been able to tell you about the delicious raspberry fool, and the fruit crumble. If it is where we think it is, it's probably situated on the upper level next to the Central Library. But if we're mistaken, you'll still find the excellent El Dorado restaurant nextdoor, which serves Mexican and Cajun food, and which does have a write-up (see below).

VEGGIES
St Mary's Place, Newcastle.
☎261 6330
Veggies operates as two restaurants in one: *day-time counter service*, open Mon–Fri, 10.30am–6.30pm, Saturday 10.30am–4.30pm; *night-time table service*, Tues–Fri 6.45–9.45pm, Saturday 4.45–9.45pm (last orders). Menu changes every day. The head chef trained in vegetarian catering at Plymouth Poly, and is primarily a vegan chef but also specialises in milk/egg based vegetarian cooking. The menu has a wide range of mostly vegan dishes: those which aren't often only differ in having cheese on top. It also appeals to non-vegetarians with original sounding dishes like pear and almond curry and white nut rissoles. A typical meal might be broccoli moussaka served with salad, and hot spiced fruit compote. Reasonably priced (about £4–£7 a head) with an informal "serve yourself" atmosphere; also student discount given.

WILLOW TEAS
St Georges Tce, Jesmond.
☎281 6874
As well as the traditional morning and afternoon tea, Willow Teas serves a range of hot and cold lunches, including some vegetarian dishes. The menu changes daily and is mostly home-style cooking like hot-

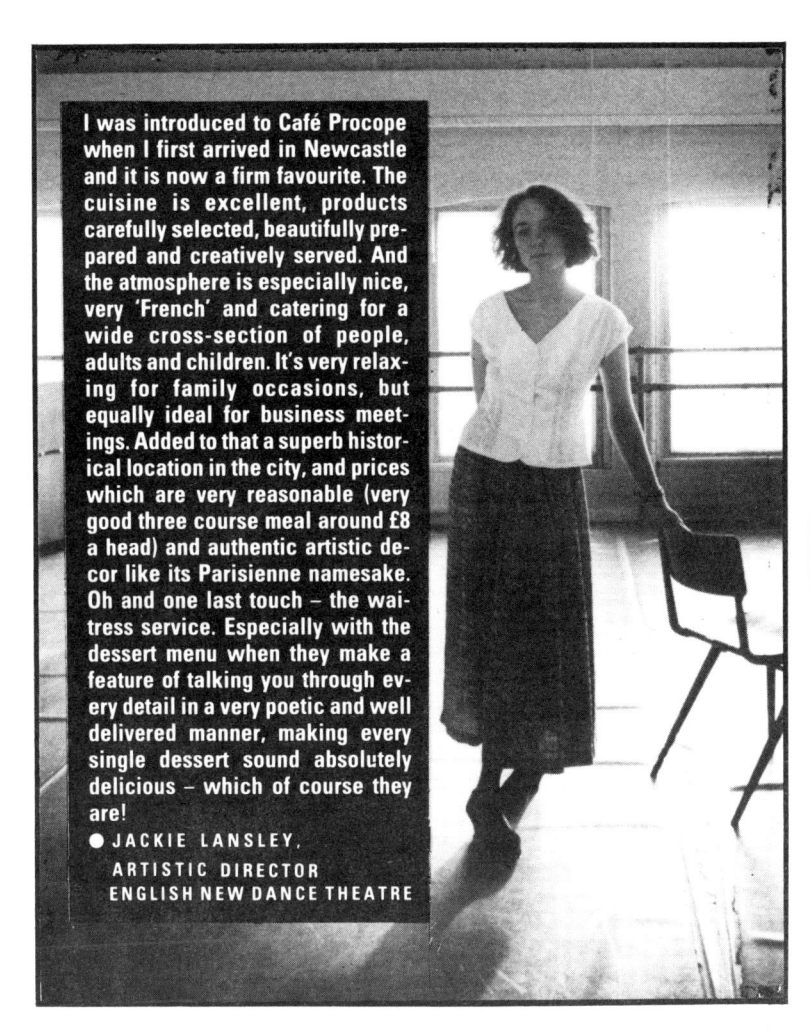

> I was introduced to Café Procope when I first arrived in Newcastle and it is now a firm favourite. The cuisine is excellent, products carefully selected, beautifully prepared and creatively served. And the atmosphere is especially nice, very 'French' and catering for a wide cross-section of people, adults and children. It's very relaxing for family occasions, but equally ideal for business meetings. Added to that a superb historical location in the city, and prices which are very reasonable (very good three course meal around £8 a head) and authentic artistic decor like its Parisienne namesake. Oh and one last touch – the waitress service. Especially with the dessert menu when they make a feature of talking you through every detail in a very poetic and well delivered manner, making every single dessert sound absolutely delicious – which of course they are!
>
> ● JACKIE LANSLEY,
>   ARTISTIC DIRECTOR
>   ENGLISH NEW DANCE THEATRE

pots, stews, and goulashes served with fresh salad and vegetables. The soup (home-made with lashings of cheese on top), and huge gooey puddings are a particular favourite! The tea-room itself is the size of a small sitting-room and often gets a little crowded! The atmosphere is warm and informal, and attracts mostly shoppers and students who use it as a popular meeting place. The prices are reasonable for lunch; soup, a main course and a pud costs around £6, but there are a lot of smaller cheaper snacks available. Paintings around the wall are usually for sale.

French

LE ROUSSILLON
St Andrews St, Newcastle.
☎261 1341
Exceedingly French, with the bar-room curtains invitingly open to prove it. The only thing not French is the chef, but he cooks from the owner's classic French book so his Englishness is almost cancelled out. The biggest cheque you could write for a meal would be around £100 for a meal for two, but, if you go for the house's finest bottle of wine, add £240. Owner Jean-Louis Sismondi comes from Monte Carlo, where he met his Ashington-born wife Christine. Jean-Louis trained in Monaco and worked for the Prince for 15 years, and there is typical French decor in the restaurant with pictures of Monaco and Paris. This is an up-market restaurant trying to reach people at large, giving good value for money and a nice relaxed atmosphere. 'My wife makes all the delectable puddings for this restaurant,' Jean-Louis says proudly. His own favourite dish is pheasant. One of our researchers had a highly sophisticated Surf and Turf meal – very Nouvelle Cuisine, with separate sauces – and her companion had a venison dish that had been marinated in Heather Whisky. Smoking is not allowed in the restaurant itself, but you can smoke in the bar.

MICHELANGELO
King St, Quayside, Newcastle.
☎261 4415
A long-established up-market French restaurant owned by four Italians. Specialities include two-person roasts from £14.50 to £19.50 and flambé steaks cooked at your table. Their delicious fish dishes range from sole fillet in white wine for £7.25 to a whole Dover sole filled with prawn and lobster sauce for £13.25. The meat dishes, all in rich sauces, start at £7.50 for veal or lamb fillet, and go up to £10.45 for Tournedos a l'escargot. If your favourite dish isn't on the menu, the chef will cook it for you. There is also a £6.50 lunchtime menu. Open: 12.30–2.15pm & 7–11pm; closed Saturday lunchtimes and all day Sundays.

RENDEZVOUS
Pink Lane, Newcastle. ☎232 6505
A bistro situated almost opposite the Central Station, with a coffee bar, a snack bar, and an ever changing blackboard menu; it's popular with theatregoers from the nearby New Tyne Theatre. Rendezvous' French atmosphere is reflected in its food, music and decor. The waitresses are attentive and anxious to please in the French fashion, but so obsessed with cleanliness that they will spray an empty table with furniture polish while people at other tables are still eating! The food prices are reasonable, and the portions can be substantial, but the house wine is an overpriced vin *ordinaire*. Two people can have a three-course meal with a litre of wine for about £25. The coffee bar has its own menu: paté, camembert, fritters, soup. Lunch: soup, venison and duck paté.

Mexican

CHI-CHI'S
Metro Centre, Gateshead.
☎460 0762
This is a Mexican restaurant situated just inside the bus station entrance to the Metro Centre. It is large and decorated to look like a Mexican courtyard. It has a very jolly atmosphere and is a good place to go with a group of friends before or after the cinema which is just beside it. All Chi-chi's food is cooked fresh to order. There is a good children's menu which is very reasonably priced, and the main menu is typically Mexican with tacos and enchiladas. Particularly recommended are the sizzling fajitas – pieces of beef or chicken cooked on a hot skillet and served with tacos and salads. There is a good sized bar with interesting drinks and cocktails and a Happy Hour. Chi-chi's is regarded as the home of Chimichanga, a Mexican speciality meat filled dish enveloped in a tortilla, deep-fried and smothered in their special seafood sauce. Every diner receives a complimentary basket of freshly cooked tortilla chips and a salsa dip (also fresh daily). Sangria is made fresh daily – at £1.50 a glass. There is live entertainment on Tuesday, Wednesday and Thursday.

EL DORADO
Princess Square, Newcastle.
☎232 9894
A friendly, intimate (i.e. small) restaurant, formerly the Latin American, now specialising in Mexican, Cajun and Creole food, a good place to go with a group of friends or for a romantic dinner for two. They offer an original, wide ranging menu of tasty, sizzling hot dishes: e.g. Veracruz fish, shark steaks, alligator kebabs (tastes a bit like fishy pork!), or buffalo-style chicken wings; desserts include pecan pie and Death by Chocolate. Don't be put off by the fact that El Dorado is hidden in the middle of the hideous concrete buildings of Princess Square – it is a delightful and innovative little restaurant that is well worth a visit. Two people can have a three-course meal, including a half litre of red wine, for around £22. It's open all day and is very busy at lunchtimes. The spring water is popular, and it also serves a wide range of cocktails, and beers including Dosequis, a special Mexican brew, and Lonestar, the national beer of Texas.

HEARTBREAK SOUP
Quayside, Newcastle. ☎222 1701
Bistro-style restaurant with Mexican decor and a regular disco held downstairs. Popular with veggies, students and young 'uns generally but used by almost everyone during the Quayside's Sunday market. Its menu is interesting and reasonably priced (£4–£7 for a main course) but the service can be a bit erratic; the chicken Jalpino is highly recommended. The Soup is rapidly becoming the trendy place to eat where you can hear very lively and sometimes quite bizarre music: the latest hit London sounds as well as Latin, hiphop, reggae etc. However, the rather casual service lets the place down: one researcher didn't get served with a main course at all one lunchtime! It stays open for food as late as midnight, and it's best to book at weekends.

ONE-EYED JACKS
Pilgrim St, Newcastle. ☎222 0130
Formerly in High Bridge, this popular restaurant now has a new home on Pilgrim Street, where Sascias used

to be. Their menu offers a wide selection of Tex Mex food: tacos, burritos, enchiladas, fujitas, chilli con carne, etc, with tortilla dips to get your palate livened up. Live music features country & western bands and singers.

Greek

ATHENEAN
St Nicholas Chambers, Amen Corner, Newcastle. ☎222 1714
This restaurant is one of the city's newest, the only Greek one. The lunch menu is fixed price and à la carte, evening à la carte only. You may start with dolmades (stuffed vine leaves), followed by spicy meat balls, finishing with ice cream and coffee, for £6.25. Or you can go à la carte with seafood platter at about £19. Although the atmosphere is quite sedate, they sometimes have live Greek music, and if they are not too busy the staff may do a Greek dance and ask you to take part. Aimed at the upper end of the market, it is very elegantly decorated with pillars, drapes from the ceiling and statuettes, and the garlanded waitresses glide barefoot across the carpet wearing slinky white robes. The room itself is large and seats 100. The traditionally Greek cuisine is notable for the tenderness of the meat, especially the lamb, which melts in your mouth. The speciality is *mezze*, a selection of Greek gourmet delights, for £12.50 a head. At lunchtimes it appeals particularly to businessmen and women; in the evenings it's a good place to go for a special night out. Open: 12.30–2.30pm & 7–11.30pm; closed Saturday lunchtime and Sunday.

German

BLACKGATE
Milburn House, Side, Newcastle.
☎261 7356
German owner Heinz Dennhofer is a well-known wine importer. Table d'hôte: five starters and five main courses. Very masculine and Germanic: wonderful for businessmen – to get their guests to start talking. The food is very tasty and characteristically German but not leaden, and the menu changes from week to week. The wine is perfect, chosen specially by the owner. Open: 12–2.30pm Mon–Fri & 7–10.30pm Tues–Sat.

American

FILLING STATION
Northumberland Rd, Newcastle.
☎232 3087
Automotive nostalgia theme restaurant derived from the conversion of an old garage in London, but with a good selection of reasonably priced food. It is a family restaurant with a special children's menu printed as a drawing and puzzle book with wax pencils – good news for harassed parents. There are separate smoking and non-smoking sections. It can be a little noisy with either American radio to listen to or videos to watch on numerous suspended televisions. The menu is mostly deep pan or thin base pizzas but there are also a few pasta dishes and an excellent self service salad

bar. The drink selection is rather restricted but includes a house wine, draught and bottled beer and the ubiquitous Coke.

HANRAHANS
Watergate Bldgs, Sandhill, Newcastle. ☎222 0164
This recently opened restaurant on the Quayside is a meat-eaters' paradise (although some salads and other veggie dishes are available), and clearly not a place for calorie counters. The most popular meals on the menu are the spare ribs and the huge 10oz steaks, both under £7 each, including various trimmings. Both restaurant and the large cocktail bar attached are always bustling, especially in the evenings. The place itself is relatively informal and has large round pine tables on which to feast and a pleasant conservatory overlooking the river. It's the second Hanrahans to be opened, the first being in Sheffield. The menu is quite wide ranging, e.g. *Starter:* Fried Mozzarella. *Main dish:* Halibut steak. *Dessert:* Rocky Mountains. The starters combine sweet and savoury tastes in an exciting way, and many people like to have two or three different ones in place of a main course. Also a large selection of German, French and Italian wines and a number of champagnes are available with priced from £5 to £45.

Thai

LOY KRATHONG
Pink St, Newcastle. ☎222 1291
A Thai restaurant with a relaxing, tropical atmosphere, complete with a traditional boxing ring. On Friday and Saturday evenings they have presentations of classical Thai dancing with beautiful girls straight out of *The King and I*. The food is based on five spices: delicate, intriguing and not a bit like Chinese food. It is traditionally eaten with the fingers but they will provide you with chopsticks or cutlery, and you can sit on the traditional seating of cushions with low teak hand-carved tables: an experience to be relished! Typical starter, dim sum (suet pastry with port and horsechestnut stuffing); main dish, prawns in chilli and sweet sauce. Set meals at £12 and £15 per head for four courses are popular. The restaurant donates some of its profits to a pet charity of the owner, Mudita, who is funding a school for children in Thailand, where English students go out to teach. There are 20 tables and you usually have to book on Friday and Saturdays; it's closed on Mondays.

HOTEL BARS & RESTAURANTS

If you're in town on a Saturday night, don't forget that Newcastle has some excellent hotel bars and restaurants which offer a quiet place for a civilised drink and meal at a time when the city centre pubs are packed with noisy revellers.

The **Royal Station Hotel**, next to Newcastle Central Station and metro, houses the elegant trattoria-style Oscars restaurant and the smart Empire bar.

Further along Neville Street on the other side of the road is the **County Hotel**, an impressive Victorian building with two restaurants and two bars, the Boston Bean Company and the Café Mozart (which has a pianist or piped classical music).

The **Swallow Hotel** above Newgate Street shopping centre is a modern high-rise hotel with a bar and restaurant on the top floor. Panoramic views of the city are a special feature of the rooftop Sharps restaurant and cocktail bar.

Four other hotels with restaurants are described in the Restaurants section of this guide: the **Crest Hotel**'s Entertainers restaurant, the Trellis Restaurant in the **Stakis Airport Hotel**, the Convivium Restaurant at the **Holiday Inn**, Seaton Burn, and the **Hospitality Inn**'s Le Jardin restaurant in Osborne Road, Jesmond.

Other Jesmond hotels with restaurants include the **Imperial Hotel** on Jesmond Road (Peacock's Restaurant), and on Osborne Road the **New Kent Hotel**, which claims to have 'possibly the finest restaurant in and around the city', and the **Ferncourt Hotel**, which has a Tex Mex restaurant called Ponchos. Another welcome oasis on Osborne Road is **Whites Hotel**, whose bar provides a comfortable place of retreat when Trotters up the road is too much of a madhouse.

MARKETS

Grainger Market: Newcastle, Mon–Sat, 9am–5pm.
Bigg Market: Newcastle, Tues, Thurs, Sat, 8am–5pm.
Quayside Market: Newcastle, Sun, 9.30am–2.30pm.
Armstrong Bridge Art & Craft Fair: Jesmond Dene, Newcastle, Sun, 9am–4pm.

Ashington: Tues, 10am–4pm.
Bedlington: Thurs, 10am–4pm.
Blyth: Tues, Fri, Sat, 7.30am–5.30pm.
Chester-le-Street: Tues, Fri, 9am–4pm.
Cramlington: Thurs, 7.30am–4pm.
Hexham: Tues, 9am–4pm.
Morpeth: Wed, 9.30–5pm.
North Shields: Mon–Sat.
South Shields: Sat, 9am–4pm.

ETHNIC FOODSTORES

As well as running numerous restaurants and corner shops, enterprising businessmen from Tyneside's various ethnic communities have in recent years opened several foodstores. At first these served the needs of their own communities, and acted wholesalers for local restaurants, with the Chinese foodstores also providing an astonishing range of other goods, from clothes to videos, for Tyneside's 4000-strong Cantonese community.

Newcastle's Chinatown restaurants then sprang up around Peter and Anne Cheng's Wing Hong supermarket in Stowell Street – almost overnight, it seemed...whereas this oriental flowering has actually taken ten years. The Cantonese love to maintain their colourful traditions, and the lion dance around Chinatown to celebrate the Chinese new year attracts bigger crowds every year. Newcastle is twinned with the town of Taiyuan in the province of Shanxi, and Newcastle Central Library recently established a Chinese section of books, tapes, videos and other resources.

The next addition to Newcastle's Chinatown will be a traditional gate across Stowell Street – not a plastic tourist replica but the real thing imported from China, constructed with special wood and a perfect painted finish.

The Japanese are the latest to make their mark on the food front with a delicatessen in Heaton, **Setsu Japan**. The local Japanese community is growing fast, with 25 Japanese firms based in the North at the last count, the highest regional concentration in Europe. Washington's Festival of the Air, the offspring of their first Japanese Kite Festival, is now firmly established favourite on the local events calendar, and it can't be too long before the first Japanese restaurant is opened on Tyneside.

Tynesiders have been converted to the joys of exotic cooking by TV cooks such as Madhur Jaffrey, Claudia Roden and Ken Hom, but they've only recently been able to buy the necessary ingredients on Tyneside. They despaired when Newcastle lost its two best delicatessens, Newmans in Clayton Street and Leathards in Jesmond, and when the short-lived Italian deli opposite the Cathedral came and went so quickly.

But now – in a league of their own – there's the **Tavasso** Italian deli in South Gosforth and **Sullivans** in Whitley Bay. And then there's always the food departments of **Fenwicks** in Newcastle and **Savacentre** (Sainsburys) at Washington, **Tiffanys** in the Galleries at Washington, and in Jesmond the recently opened **Jesmond Delicatessen** on Jesmond Road and **Country Whey** on Clayton Road.

On the wholefood front there are many small healthfood shops scattered around Tyneside, and several good ones in Newcastle, notably **Mandala** in Manor House Road, Jesmond, **Red Herring** in Studley Terrace, Fenham, **Almonds & Raisins** in Queens Square and Eldon Garden, **The Bean Pot** on Lower Westgate Road, **Health Fayre** in St Mary's Place, and a branch of **Holland & Barrett** in the Bigg Market.

As well as the ethnic foodstores listed below, many Asian cornershops have well-stocked ethnic food sections, notably **Continental Foodstores** at the junction of Osborne Avenue and Jesmond Road.

Brighton Oriental Food Store (16–18 Brighton Grove, Fenham, Newcastle. ☎273 1070). This is an excellent shop for fresh Indian herbs, spices, all kinds of unusual and continental fruit and vegetables, and many different kinds of rice. The bags of little 'indescribables' are popular with Fenham students and other shoppers, and the pakoras, at 50p for a big bag, make a delicious snack. It is probably the Indian sweetmeats and sticky titbits which are most sought after in Fenham, and if you are not sure what anything tastes like you are always allowed a little pick before you buy anything too unrecognisable! The shop also sells halal meat.

Eastern Pearl (27 Fenkle St, Newcastle. ☎261 5623). Similar to the larger Wing Hong Supermarket, with an excellent selection of woks, steamers and Chinese cookery implements for those who like to approach their Chinese cookery with style. They also have some interesting bottles of Saki, and Chinese wines for authentic tastes. An unexpected item is a range of pretty Chinese slippers.

Setsu Japan (196a Heaton Road, Heaton, Newcastle. ☎265 9970). This is the first Japanese food shop in the North East, and has such a well-stocked range of oriental delicacies – from octopus to zushi – that it is also able to operate a delivery service to Scotland and various parts of England. There is fresh meat for sukiyaki, fresh fish for sashimi, and many dry and frozen foods (all sealed in brightly coloured wrappers blazoned with baffling Japanese script!), as well as Japanese tableware and cooking utensils. A takeaway service is available between 11am and 1pm on Saturday and Sunday lunchtimes for maki-zushi and inari-zushi. They also specialise in banquet catering, supplying Japanese dishes to order and special conference lunch boxes. Other facilities include a Japanese video club and cheap London-Japan air tickets.

Sullivans (152 Park View, Whitley Bay. ☎252 1125). A long narrow shop stocked with every imaginable delight from floor to high ceiling: excellent selections of cooked meat and cheeses, beautiful home-made fresh crab paté and delicious ice cream. An old-fashioned, courteous shop, not a place to rush into if you're in a hurry: just stand in the queue, savour the atmosphere, and cast your eyes over the shelves – where you'll discover the kinds of things you'd long given up hope of finding anywhere.

Tavasso (2 Newlands Road, South Gosforth, Newcastle. ☎285 4052). The Sparacios' recently established Italian delicatessen sells prepared food and all kinds of Italian produce: cheeses, cooked meats, fresh pasta, sauces, cakes, rice, biscuits, Italian wines, liqueurs and beers, some of these not available anywhere else in the North East. The wines include some excellent ones which you won't find at any off licence. The shop has a wonderful Italian atmosphere and *smell*, and Mary and Nicky Sparacio will tell you what everything is and make up the most delicious sauces to order. They also do home deliveries and catering. Open: 9.30am–6pm daily, and till 7pm on Fridays.

Wah Fung Hong Supermarket (87 Percy St, Newcastle. ☎232 7965). Stocks many of the items sold by the other Chinatown supermarkets, with lovely and unusual items like Chinese cucumbers (look a bit like ours, but more oriental), sweet yams, and plenty of fascinating notices giving details of where to train in karate and tai chi quan. There's also an attractive range of Chinese dolls and ornaments, including some of Hong Kong river floats.

Wing Hong Supermarket (45 Stowell St, Newcastle. ☎261 2630). This is an experience. Sundays are like United Nations days, with fascinated, if sometimes puzzled, English customers, rubbing shoulders with both traditional and integrated modern Chinese, amidst a cornucopia of delightful foodstuffs. These include dim sum, dried fish, prawns, oysters, duck, Chinese greens, impressively large Spanish onions, and all kinds of interesting oriental canned foods. Don't be put off by the catering-size packs of vegetables: the Chinese believe in pleasing any customer and are happy to let you have a small portion. This is also a mecca for items like bottles of soy sauce and other Chinese sauces for those who have solved the mysteries of wok cookery, and there are whole ranges of bowls, china spoons, teapots and tiny cups.

METROCENTRE

The MetroCentre is Europe's largest out-of-town shopping and leisure centre. Extending over two million square feet, it has three miles of shopping malls and more than 300 shops.

You really need the best part of a day to explore the whole centre. Although it is clearly divided into four colour-coded quadrants, and there are maps everywhere, the sheer size of the place means that specific shops are sometimes hard to find. The air-conditioning and natural light do, however, make it a very comfortable environment – much airier and pleasanter in our opinion than Newcastle's rival Eldon Square.

There's a wide selection of shops, from department stores to designer boutiques, and there are also areas of shops grouped to a theme, such as the olde worlde style of Antique Court, the Roman Forum, the Garden Court, and the new Mediterranean Village.

Shopping isn't the only attraction either, with more than 40 places to eat, a ten-screen cinema, GX Superbowl (a 28-lane bowling alley), and MetroLand, Europe's only indoor theme park. This indoor funfair, set out as the fairytale Kingdom of King Wiz, has ten different playground rides including the Galaxy Express roller coaster and the Flying Galleon, a 'Video Academy' with 85 different electronic games, a 3D cinema and a nine-hole mini-golf course. There's no entrance fee – you pay as you ride – but you can get an all day pass for £3.50.

There's late night shopping in Newcastle on Thursdays, but the MetroCentre shops are open every weekday evening, from 10am till 8pm (9pm on Thursdays) and from 9am till 6pm on Saturdays, and there are 10,000 free car parking spaces. The cinemas and many of the eating places stay open after the shops have closed.

Three miles south-west of Newcastle on the A69 (a fast dual carriageway), it's easy to reach by car, and there are regular bus services from all areas and a shuttle service from Newcastle's (Grey's) Monument every few minutes. It also has its own taxi firm, and you can call for a cab from a free telephone on one of the shopping malls. The railway station links it to Newcastle, Carlisle, Durham, Wearside and Teesside, with 60 trains stopping every day (it's only seven minutes from Newcastle Central Station).

Tynesiders love to throw coins into the MetroCentre's many

pools and fountains, and all this money pays for the wheelchairs which are freely available from the Information Centre. The entrances were designed with the elderly and disabled in mind, and there are more than 100 car parking spaces for the disabled. Another welcome facility is the Playland Creche, where qualified nursery staff look after children from one to seven years old. However, pets aren't permitted in the MetroCentre: the only animals allowed are guide dogs.

Owned by the Church Commissioners, the MetroCentre was turned from what many thought was a pie in the sky dream into one of the North's great success stories by Tyneside businessman John Hall and Cameron Hall Developments.

MetroCentre Information: ☎091–460 5299.

MetroEaters

Round the World in Ate-y Days!

You may wonder how this vast centre manages to support so many different kinds of food outlets – over 40 at the latest count – but it continues to do so, with more on the way. Twelve restaurants make up the American-style **Clockworks** where you can eat American, Italian, Chinese or English food in a communal seating area.

Elsewhere, as well as the familiar **Wimpy, McDonalds** and **Pizza Hut** chain outlets, there are a number of interesting, individual eateries, serving everything from Italian ice cream to squidgy cream cakes. The major MetroCentre department stores have their own cafés, including **Gateway** (Red Balloon cafeteria), **BHS** (a café and a patio restaurant), **Littlewoods** (Picnic Basket), **Sears** (the Circle designer café), **Marks & Spencer** (The Garden) and **House of Fraser** (Continental Café).

One of the best new restaurants on Tyneside is **Chi-Chi's** Mexican restaurant in the MetroCentre, described in the Restaurants section of this guide. Among the latest MetroCentre openings are Tyneside's third Thai restaurant, the **Star of Siam** and an American 1920s restaurant/bar/nightclub complex, **Harveys**.

Here's a taste of where you can eat at the MetroCentre:

Harveys is named after the man who, instead of leaping off a skyscraper in New York in 1929 when Wall Street crashed, invented the Harvey Wallbanger cocktail and made another fortune. In a 1920s-style setting complete with a copy of the Statue of Liberty you can eat everything from fish dishes to pastas, pizzas and sandwiches, and the house speciality is a cocktail which costs £100. However, it does serve up to eight people and comes with all the trimmings including smoked salmon titbits. The finger food menu includes potato skins (crispy baked skins loaded with a choice of sour cream or chilli tomato dip), Egyptian Chicken (marinated in olive oil and garlic), char-grilled shark steak and Mum's Fruit Pie.

Star of Siam offers delicate Thai dishes with their subtle spicy tastes blended from a mixture of herbs and spices. Run by Thai businessman Manit Limratana (who has a newsagent's in Blackhall) with his Geordie-born wife Kathryn, the Star is a 100-seater restaurant staffed by Thais, with a bar and bar meals available as well as the restaurant cuisine.

American fast food is the order of much of the day in the Metrocentre, with Yankee-style serveries, complete with young Geordies telling you to 'have a nice day', simultaneously serving up hotdogs, popcorn, nachos and baked potatoes. These include **Hollywood Express**, and a similar operation just inside the foyer of the AMC multi-screen cinema. Prices from about 90p upwards.

Clockworks is another American-style import: a dozen different eating outlets in a circle surrounded by all kinds of real clocks, including grandfathers, tilted at alarming angles on the walls, and a larger than life clock interior which plays merrily every half hour. There are different eating styles and ethnic foods available, so you can choose what you want, then join your friends at tables in the communal dining area. Downstairs is a non-smoking area; smokers have their tables upstairs by the bar, just around from the carvery. Here's a selection of Clockworks eateries:

Pier 17: English grub, with a choice of fish main course between £2.45 and £2.95. Soup 65p, soft drinks and beverages available.
Pizza and Pasta: Top price £2.05 for spaghetti bolognaise or a hot pizza.
Burgerworks: Flame-grilled burgers made from 100% beef, e.g. bacon and Swiss cheese, £1.70; or a quarter pounder cheeseburger with chips, £2.55.
Le Papillon: Croissants, cakes, scones, and cinnamon shakes (rolls sprinkled with cinnamon).
Serendipity: Ice cream parlour with soft drinks and coffee.
60 Second Street: Espresso 55p a cup; cappuccino 65p a cup. Sandwiches made to order with a choice of 30 different fillings from cottage cheese to smoked salmon.
Wok 'n' Roll: A Chinese-owned eatery where the food is ready cooked. Chopsticks are provided, but not small bowls to eat the food from. A whole range of choice, with the cheapest meal being £2.05 for a vegetarian curry.
La Colonnade Carvery: On the balcony area, where you can eat beef and Yorkshire pudding, pork with apple sauce or turkey with cranberry sauce as a meal or settle for a hot meat sandwich ranging from £1.95 up to £3.95 (very substantial). Bar available, with a range of cocktails, and smoking is allowed.

Berkeley Square is a reasonably priced eating place which started off as little more than a snack bar, and now offers possibly the best Metro-Centre ice cream deal with a generous serving on a cornet, which is dipped in a flavoured sherbert topping of your choice and topped with a chocolate bar for just 30p. It also serves coffees, scones, sandwiches.

La Colonnade has enormous main course salads for £2.15 with a choice of dressings. Super sandwiches including smoked salmon and a choice of hot dishes including chef's special of the day, e.g. chilli con carne with rice and garlic bread for £2.85.

Massarellas serves Italian food along with some typical English dishes including Toad in the Hole for £1.75; steak and kidney pie, £2.95; mince and dumplings, £2.65; and roast pork with trimmings £3.85. There's also a Massarellas Gelateria along the gallery selling unusual flavoured ice cream.

Gateways Red Balloon Restaurant is a busy cafeteria with different hot and cold counters where you can choose your own dishes. Includes £2.15 three-course special lunch of soup, a choice of hot dishes and a dessert, as well as a hearty breakfast (9–10.45am) of bacon, egg, sausage, sauté potatoes, beans or tomatoes and coffee or tea for £1.35.

Choux Shop is the place for a wicked selection of gateaux, creamy cakes and puddings; jacket potatoes from £1.20 with a choice of fillings; lasagne and salad, £2.50; and bacon and ham pie with salad £2.45.

Foodles: Enormous bap sandwiches customer-built to order including veggie salad, £2.15; hot chicken, £1.35; hot bacon, 95p; and prawn, £1.75. A meal in themselves.

Sweet Temptations is where to indulge yourself with home-baked cakes, scones and fancies. Set in a lovely position in Antiques Court, its outside café tables are next to the bridge and waterwheel over the real stream that runs through it. Coffee and cheesecake from £1.10; fancy cakes, two for 50p.

Metromunch: is the first eating place you see when you arrive at the bus station entrance. Special OAP's meal with chips at £1.75, or hot pizza for £2.

Marks & Spencer's Garden holds the distinction of being the only instore M&S restaurant. It's a delightfully decorated green restaurant (no smoking permitted anywhere) serving the kind of dishes they sell in their food department which has earned an entry in Egon Ronay's *Just a Bite* food guide.

> We went to Michelangelo's the first week it opened and were probably the only two people there. We found the food, atmosphere and service excellent and have always used the restaurant ever since. We have tried many other places, but we cannot find what we want and always return to Michelangelo's when we want a nice evening out.
> ● JOHN HALL, BUSINESSMAN (METROCENTRE)

RESTAURANTS   99

ELDON SQUARE

When it was built, Newcastle's Eldon Square was the largest indoor shopping centre in Britain, one of Europe's biggest. It has over 120 shops on two levels including some of Tyneside's finest department stores, such as Bainbridge and Fenwicks (which juts into it), the biggest Boots in the region, and the adjoining Marks & Spencers, the largest M&S store outside London.

From Northumberland Street it stretches around the old Eldon Square, with one leg reaching W.H. Smith's at Grey's Monument and another taking in the Greenmarket, which houses numerous fruit and vegetable shops, and the new Eldon Food Court. Above the Nelson Street entrance is the huge Eldon Square Recreation Centre, where more than 16,000 people a week use a wide range of sports and leisure facilities. A new offshoot across Percy Street is the Eldon Garden.

Eldon Square has its metro station (Monument), a bus station underneath, and two multi-storey car parks. It's used by an estimated 25 million visitors a year. Its opening hours are 9am to 5.30pm, Monday to Saturday, with late night shopping on Thursdays till 9pm.

● Used by 25 million people a year, Newcastle's Eldon Square has several department stores, as well as restaurants, pubs, cafés, a sports complex and over 100 smaller shops.

ELDON FOOD COURT
Fast food from round the world

The Food Court has nine different food outlets. Like the rival Clockworks at the MetroCentre, it is a collection of eateries with food from different countries, with seating for 500 people. A main course from most will cost you about £2.

The Court has a plasticky but clean decor, with small tables and rather uncomfortable chairs, some of which are like park benches. It's quite airy, but the ever-present schmaltzy muzak makes it about as relaxing as a supermarket. The accent is on speed, and the cleaners tend to dust you down at the same time as the tables. It's not the sort of places to take visiting VIPs to impress them, whatever your status in life!

The toilets, however, are ultra-clean, and won first prize in the regional section of the Loo of the Year Award for 1988. Mothers will find a baby change place where they can feed and change their youngsters in comfort, and there are also plans afoot for Eldon Food Court children's parties.

Here's a round-up of what's on offer around the Court:

Trawlers: Around £2 a head for fish and chips of the 'secret of success is in the batter' variety. Not just the usual cod or haddock, but several different fish dishes. Very popular with the shoppers: fish and chips has always been an essential element in the Geordie diet.
Sweet 'n' Sour: Fast food Chinese. Not everyone's idea of Chinese cuisine, but acceptable. They do provide chopsticks, but not small bowls to eat the food from, which rather defeats the purpose. The menu includes spicy Malaysian chicken curry and Satay beef, and the cheapest meal is vegetarian curry at £2.05; also jasmine tea.
The Italian: Pizzas, pasta, ice cream, cappuccino and espresso.
Dinner Jackets: All kinds of baked stuffed potatoes at an average of £2.50 per head.
Northern Pantry: Freshly baked pies, peas and chips; chef's special steak and kidney pie, mince pie, around £1.95.
The Grill: One cheap meal here is pastie, chips and beans for £1.75. It shares a kitchen with its parent Northern Pantry nextdoor.
Picnic Basket: Supposed to offer a taste of the country – seasonal salads and sandwiches, quiches, wholemeal buns filled with hot roast beef or pork (£1.65).
The Ranch: Tex Mex, a sort of Yankee/Mexican mish mash of food to which Tyneside is now accustomed. Chef's special is a jaw-breaking cheeseburger for £1.75: try stretching your mouth wide enough to wide enough to take a bite from it!
Patisserie: Specialising in Danish pastries and cakes including Stefanka ('a Polish specialilty'), cheesecake, doughnuts, meringues, etc; also cappuccino and espresso.

ELDON GARDEN
A taste of France from Scotland

Le Café Noir in Eldon Garden is part of a Scottish chain of licensed French café/brasseries designed with the French Art Deco period in mind.

The café is open from 9am, serving continental breakfasts and coffee. The patisserie menu is available all day: croissants, baguettes, scones, pancakes, gateaux, speciality teas and hot chocolate. There is also a cold salad bar from 12 noon until late, serving a range of continental cold meats, quiches, baked potatoes and salads.

On the balcony level in Le Café Noir is a bistro open from 12 till 2.30pm for lunch and from 5 till 11pm for dinner. With seating for 60 people, there is a table d'hôte and an à la carte menu. The bistro is open all day on Saturdays.

Manners, the well-known local butchers, now have a shop on the ground floor of Eldon Garden. As well as selling their wide range of meat and poultry, their shop has a small delicatessen counter. **Almonds & Raisins**, the excellent health food shop already trading in Queen's Square, has a new branch nextdoor, while **Mistletoe Bakery** from Jesmond provides all the different cakes and breads you'd expect to find in one of the area's most popular bakeries as well as a special bake-to-order service for cakes. They reckon they can produce just about everything from a Thomas the Tank Engine birthday cake to a special personalised wedding cake.

The top floor of Eldon Garden has a Dickensian-theme coffee house and ice cream parlour called **Copperfields**, situated on the bridge over Percy Street, serving such items as Waistcoat Fillers from the Dingley Dell Bakehouse (scones, muffins, crumpets and teacakes), Copperfields stotties, Mr Micawber's toasties and 'Dickensian Specialities' (coffee with ice cream and cinnamon or hot chocolate with cream and chocolate flake).

PICK OF THE SARNIE SHOPS

Tyneside, home of the stottie, is surprisingly unimaginative when it comes to tasty lunchtime snacks and sandwiches. The general menu is very much limited to 'cheese and coleslaw or ham salad', often with either no butter or with catering-quality margarine. Many use tasteless, often dry white bread, running out of brown rolls and stotties quickly, and not learning the obvious lesson from this: that office workers, at least, are conscious that white bread is less nutritious than brown, and that if you do eat white bread there are some tasty varieties to be had from the region's better bakers. There's certainly little to compare here with the plethora of tiny back-street sandwich shops in London, which offer a huge variety of delicious and exotic fillings. There are, however, a few exceptions:

Health Fayre on the Haymarket do a nice peanut butter and banana, or date and cream cheese stottie (brown). **Olivers** gives good value, and **Next** is worth a visit, if only for one of their delicious hot beef sandwiches (£2.10), almost a meal in itself; they also have a slimmer's special for £2.40, one of which is filled with prawns, melon and fresh salad.

The best sandwich shop is in a league of its own. **Supersnack**, on Mosley Street, is easily spotted at lunchtime by the long queue of people straining their necks to see if the last Chicken Breast Club (chicken, salami, cheese, salad and mayo for a mere 80p) has gone. Fillings include lamb tikka, spicey chicken, North Sea prawn salad, rainbow trout, Brie and peaches, sausage and chilli relish – in white finger rolls, brown buns, white baps, brown "torpedoes", or stotties. If you're still hungry, try a vegetable samosa, an apple strudel or a fresh cream strawberry tart.

The **Jumbo Baked Potato Shop** in Ridley Place, as well as serving an inventive range of fillings for jacket potatoes, specialises in stotties bulging with such things as bacon and cheese omelette, mushroom omelette and Waldorf salad. The nearby **Breadcrumbs** on Northumberland Road does enormous hot stotties filled with bacon, egg, beans, sausage, etc. It also has a sit-down area much used by shoppers and students, and the walls are covered with posters advertising forthcoming events on the arty/student circuit. The teapots are large and are constantly refilled, and it's open from 8.30am till 6pm.

Round the corner in Ridley Place, **The Bookhouse** has a busy little coffee bar in the basement where you can have a cup of real Italian espresso with a toastie, followed by home-baked American chocolate brownies, while pondering what books, postcards or gifts you should buy from the shop upstairs.

Down on the Quayside the oddly named **Country Fare** (beneath the Tyne Bridge) is just about the best place in the area for a gut-busting grease-out. The traditional sandwiches tend to be rather ordinary, but the chip butties are something else, and you can have a quarter or a *half* stotty filled with bacon, eggs, beans and tomato, or grilled mushrooms with cheese. There are also a few tables where you can sit down with a cup of tea and a plate of chips, or a full cooked breakfast (available until the afternoon).

If you like the stotties they sell on the Newcastle-London shuttle buses, go to **Jack's Snacks** in Grantham Road, Sandyford, stotty supplier to many offices as well as the buses and a favourite port of call for police patrol cars. **Alice's Kitchen** round the corner in Helmsley Road is another good place for stotties.

Finally, for vegetarians and others who like eating things which are supposed to be good for you, the **Bean Pot** on Lower Westgate Road has fresh salad stotties and sandwiches smeared with nutritious veggie spreads containing herbs and other strange-tasting concoctions. As well as loaves of their own bread, they also sell the usual range of wholefood products. Situated in a time-warp in Newcastle Arts Centre, the shop has a soporific, worthy atmosphere; the staff are very earnest, and you feel they would be visibly shocked if someone walked in with a pound of sausages.

CLUBLAND

A traditional Geordie night out

Regional clubland has launched some of the biggest household names on the road to success on both stage and TV. International magician Paul Daniels, singers Paul Squires and Leah Bell, comedy stars like Ken Dodd, Bernard Manning, Chubby Brown, pop musicians like the Animals, AC/DC and Sting all started their climb up the showbiz ladder by taking their first step entertaining in social clubs.

They have obviously gone a long way since then but still make the occasional appearance back in their grass roots territory. And North-East clubland is the very heart of the social club movement in Britain and an area where visitors are sure to find a warm welcome. No other region anywhere in Britain can offer the traveller so much. There are 800 clubs in the region, and the biggest branch in the Club and Institute Union is Durham, the stronghold with 310 clubs. They include some of the most lavish in the country and offer their members not only a meeting place for a social drink, but facilities and entertainment that are unrivalled.

The clubs have three main features. Firstly the bar, often combined with sporting and games facilities for darts, dominoes, whist, crib, pool, snooker, skittles, and chess within the club, and soccer, golf, angling, quoits, bowls, pigeon racing and whippet racing outdoors.

The other two cater for those less active clubmen and their wives who may want to simply enjoy a drink and a chat in the luxury of a lounge that may well rival the best hotels, or who want to enjoy a pint and be entertained while doing so, or even join in a game of bingo.

The CIU clubs will welcome all associate members, who only need to sign the visitors' book to be admitted. But if you're not a member of a CIU you should contact the secretary of the club you are intending to visit. If you're not signed in as a visitor, you may well be refused entry. Indeed, regular visitors to the area may well find it an advantage to become members of a club.

It is simply a matter of finding a couple of members to propose and second you as a member. Club officials are usually delighted to put your name on a proposal form. The cost is very little and having a membership and a national pass card means you'll be welcome at clubs throughout the land as you travel the country. Both Northumberland CIU branch secretary Ernie Moore (☎285 1478) and his Durham counterpart Jack Amos (☎Durham 386 3921) will help by suggesting an appropriate club and even possibly introducing a visitor as a member.

As a guide to the top clubs, the region boasts four who have been Supreme Club of Great Britain: **Cramlington High Pit**, **Newcastle RAOB**, Gateshead **Stormont Main** and **Innisfree Catholic Club** at Longbenton. One of the busiest town centre clubs is **Newcastle Labour Club**, opened only ten years ago, and where Lord Mayors and top regional trade union officials are among the membership. It is a really big club and one where members can pop in for a rest while doing their shopping or where workers can drop by for a lunchtime drink.

On the northern outskirts of the city, **Westerhope Comrades** is another big club with exceptional facilities. The region's last big club to be built was **Jarrow Ellison SC** on South Tyneside.

A guide to the clubs mentioned is given below, but a quick glance at Yellow Pages will show the full range of the clubs both large and small throughout the area.

Cramlington High Pit SC, High Pit, Cramlington. ☎0670–713108.
Newcastle RAOB SC, 22 Heaton Rd, Newcastle. ☎265 5550.
Stormont Main WMC, 10 Springwell Rd, Wrekenton, Gateshead. ☎487 5224.
Innisfree SC, Chesters Ave, Longbenton Estate, Newcastle. ☎266 2503.
Newcastle Labour Club, Leazes Park Road, Newcastle. ☎232 8049.
Westerhope Comrades SC, Trevelyan Drive, Westerhope. ☎286 0410.
Jarrow Ellison SC, Ellison St, Jarrow. ☎489 7267.
Ashington Comrades SC, 183 North Seaton Rd, Ashington. ☎0670–814007.
Coxlodge Gosforth SC, Park House, Jubilee Rd, Gosforth. ☎285 6916.
Percy Main SC, 4 Norham Rd, Percy Main, North Shields. ☎257 1749.

Throckley Union Jack SC, Hilda Tce, Throckley. ☎267 4669.
Chilton & Windlestone SC, Darlington Rd, Chilton, Ferryhill. ☎0388–720294.
Consett Victoria SC, Gloucester Rd, Consett. ☎0207–503758.
Farrington SC, Anthony Rd, Sunderland. ☎528 0517.
Leam Lane SC, Fewster Sq, Felling, Gateshead. ☎469 3484.
North Biddick SC, Front St, Fatfield, Washington. ☎416 0148.
Osborne WMC, Osborne Rd, Chester-le-Street. ☎388 3003.
Ryton SC, Dean Tce, Ryton. ☎413 2308.
Usworth & District SC, Manor Rd, Washington. ☎416 2978.
Usworth & Washington Gardeners SC, Industrial Rd, Washington ☎416 0472.
Simonside SC, 197 Winskell Rd, South Shields. ☎455 3780.

NIGHTCLUBS

Stepping out on Tyneside

As you'd expect for a regional capital, Tyneside has a wide range of nightclubs catering for all ages and all styles – and almost all night long.

ANNABELS
High St West, Sunderland.
☎565 9117
Now in a new location, Annabels caters for 18 to 30 year olds, with a capacity of 350. A membership is required for entrance: obtainable free any evening at the club, but before 10pm. Open Mon, Wed, Thurs, Fri and Sat. Non-members £1 admission, Mon, Wed and Thurs. Entrance costs £3 on Friday and Saturday regardless of membership. Annabels has four bars, one of which is situated in the restaurant and serves a wide range of food. The DJs play various kinds of music, from jazz to the latest chart hits. Annabels also cater for private parties – usually on Mondays, Wednesdays and Thursdays – and tickets are provided free of charge.

BENTLEYS
Cloth Market, Newcastle.
☎261 5780
Bentleys plays music for the Bigg Market crowd: the latest chart and dance hits. Open till 2am, there's no membership needed for four nights a week, but Mondays and Wednesdays are private party nights. Tues & Thurs: £1.50; Fri, £1 before 10.30pm, £3 after; Sat, £1.50 before 10.30pm, £3 after. Hamburgers, chips, pizzas and toasties are available during the week. Formerly *Reflections*, it's still an informal club, with no dress restrictions.

THE COOPERAGE
The Close, Quayside, Newcastle.
☎232 8286
Upstairs in the famous Quayside pub is a disco open to the public for three nights a week. There are live bands on alternate Thursday nights (price depends on who's playing); Friday & Saturday disco, members £1 & guests £1.25 before 10.30pm, 50p extra after. Mon–Wed, private parties. Not your usual Newcastle nightspot: the beer is excellent and not overpriced, the bar food isn't bad, the music is a mixture of Motown and student favourites, the doormen are human, and most of the clientele have an IQ higher than their age. Dress: jeans and leather jackets preferred by most, but optional. Decor: about 600 years old, like the building.

THE COTTON CLUB
High Street, Gateshead. ☎477 7334
Open to customers of all ages, from 18 to 50. This is a large club on two floors: upstairs is mainly for 18 year olds; downstairs for more mature night owls, with two bars, one in the restaurant area, serving things like chip butties and pizzas. Live acts are provided but generally for private parties, which cost nothing to arrange. Open from 7pm seven days a week: Mon, Thurs, Fri, Sat, till 1am; Tues, Wed, till 11pm; Sunday, till 10.30pm. Free entrance till 9pm when a fee of £1.50 is charged. The music varies depending on the day of

the week: Mondays to Thursdays the music is very mixed ranging from 50s to today's pop charts, and on Fridays and Saturdays the music tends to cater for the visitors who enjoy soul and house music.

GREYS CLUB
Grey St, Newcastle. ☎261 4066
Greys Club is open to the over 25s: membership is free with a 48 hours acceptance period. Entrance is free to members from Tuesday to Thursday, or £2 to guests. Visits on Friday and Saturday will cost members £2.50 and guests £3.50. The music here is variable and sandwiches are available from either of the two bars. It's a small intimate club that generally caters for the mature end of the market.

HOBOS
Bath Lane, Newcastle. ☎232 3803
Hobo's is an up-market club open to members only. Membership costs vary from the type of card you require. A red membership costs £9.80 a year which allows you free entrance up to 10pm, then a charge of £3 after this time. A silver membership costs £40 a year, which gives you free entrance until 11pm, then £2 after. A gold membership costs £250 per year and entrance is free at all times with 10 guests per member. Open from Tues–Sat, 7pm–3am. No live acts or music are provided, just DJs and disco. The club has two bars plus a cocktail bar, and there's also an à la carte restaurant providing excellent food, with two musicians providing pleasant background music. Music covers the whole board every evening, and private parties are catered for at the manager's discretion. Wednesday night is student night: the Breakfast Club.

JULIES
The Close, Quayside, Newcastle.
☎232 7240
Small and friendly with a great party atmosphere, Julies is mainly a soul music club, open on Tuesday, Thursday, Friday and Saturday nights, attracting all kinds of people but young people especially on Saturdays. Admission is £2 during the week and £3 on Fridays and Saturdays, and jeans are acceptable.

MADISONS
New Bridge St, Newcastle.
☎232 4910
A large club above the Crest Hotel with a capacity of 1000, Madisons is open to the general public with no membership requirement. The entrance fee on Monday, Tuesday and Wednesday is £2, £2.50 on Thursday, £3 before 11pm and £3.50 after 11pm on Friday and £4 all night on Saturday. There is an added bonus for holders of student union cards. On Mondays to Thursdays, entrance is free. There are occasional live acts but general music is operated by two DJs. Monday evening is student night, with alternative music. Tuesday and Thursdays are called party nights with the DJs providing lots of fun and games, usually catering for birthdays. Wednesday is a soul, funk and jazz evening and on Fridays and Saturdays you can expect to find jazz and soul in the small disco and mixed music on the large dance floor. With its five bars, one a cocktail bar, and its English/Italian restaurant, Madisons provides triple entertainment for all kinds of people.

MAYFAIR
Newgate St, Newcastle.
☎232 3109
Open Tuesdays, Fridays and Saturdays. Fridays and Saturdays are rock nights, with entry free before 10pm

CLUBS 107

Three pubs to have a social drink in unpretentious surroundings: the Free Trade Inn (St Lawrence), the Ship Inn (Stepney Bank) and the Tap & Spile (Byker). For music, go to the Riverside (Melbourne Street) to see every up-and-coming band worth checking out. For nosh, go the the pricey (but great for vegetable dishes) Sachins Punjabi restaurant or Francescas Italian restaurant in Jesmond for a good helping of vegetarian cannelloni or lasagne in a very busy and very jolly atmosphere.
● MARTIN BRAMMER, MUSICIAN (THE KANE GANG)

if you're a member. Membership is £2 a year. Tuesdays is Big Band night when there is ballroom dancing to a five-piece band. On Thursdays there are various functions for students, with no dress restrictions. The Mayfair is also a regular venue for touring rock and pop groups.

RIVERSIDE
Melbourne St, Newcastle.
☎261 4386
The North East's premier venue for local and big name live bands. It has a capacity of 450, but still has an intimate and casual atmosphere. It's a members only club, with over 6000 members, and is open till midnight, with free admission before 9pm on some nights. On Fridays there is an independent music disco; on Saturdays a dance-house music disco. It has all kinds of live events, from rock to jazz to African to folk etc, often four or five times a week. In only its second year Riverside was voted the second-best music venue outside London by NME readers. Run by a youthful co-operative, it has a policy of providing a platform for local musicians, with over 1000 local bands appearing in its first four years. It also hosts the regional heats of Radio One's *Musical Style* competition to find the best new band in Britain and of BBC Television's *Saturday Superstore* talent competition. It has rehearsal rooms for local musicians, and Sound Advice, a computerised information service for and about the music industry.

ROCKSHOTS
Waterloo St, Newcastle.
☎232 9648
The busiest night club in Newcastle. Rockshots is predominantly a gay club but welcomes anyone. A membership is required for entrance but this is free to students and gay visitors and holders of ordinary gold

cards. The concessionary card available for regulars costs £20 for the first year, and then £15 a year. Open Monday to Saturday, 10.30pm–2am, and Friday and Saturday lunchtimes, 12.30–3pm. The charges for entrance are: Monday and Wednesday, members free, guest £1.50; Tuesday, members £1, guests £2; Thursday and Friday, members £1.50, guests £2.50; Saturday, members £2.50, guests £4.50 guests. Lunchtimes: members £1, guests £1.50. Live acts appear on Mondays and Saturdays, ranging from the blue humour of Chubby Brown to chart topper Hazel Dean. Female strippers disrobe on Friday and Saturday afternoons, and male strippers on the first Wednesday of every month, which is a male only night. Rockshots has two bars and a snack bar serving burgers and chips etc. The music at Rockshots matches its brilliant lightshow. You can find anything from 50s jazz to today's chart hits on Tuesdays and Thursdays, which are student/"straight" nights, and mostly high energy, beat and Acid House on other nights. Private parties are usually held on Monday, Tuesday, and Wednesday nights, with tickets issued at no extra cost unless a buffet or live act is required.

RUPERTS
Ocean Rd, South Shields.
☎456 5801
A small club where the music is the latest pop and dance chart sounds, except on Tuesday, which is heavy metal night. Admission: Mon, £1.80; Tues–Thurs, £2; Fri & Sat, £2.50. Popular with locals, Ruperts is particularly busy on Friday nights. Drinks at the three bars are reasonably priced, as is the food – chicken & chips, burger & chips, etc. The club appeals to everyone from 19 to 50, and has one of the few female club DJs on Tyneside.

SANDS
Park Ave, Whitley Bay. ☎253 0420
This popular Coast nightspot is a private members club: you have to be signed in by a member, or wait 48 hours for membership to be processed. It's open on Mondays and Thursdays (over-21s, entry £1), Fridays and Saturdays (£1.30 10–11pm, £2.30 11–12pm, no admission after 12pm).

STAGE DOOR
Stowell St, Newcastle. ☎232 2313
The 'Stagey' is a favourite haunt for university students and locals who don't want to walk too far for a dance after the pubs close. Although there's usually a queue, there are no dress restrictions and the atmosphere is unpretentious and friendly. The disco area is small and sweaty, and the music is mostly nostalgic 70s and 80s hits. There's an upstairs bar with a jukebox used by a strange mixture of Sloane Rangerish rugby playing students and their female counterparts, bus drivers and older blokes looking for love. This is the place to go if you are a collector of corny chat-up lines like 'You don't sweat much for a fat lass.'

THE STUDIO
New Bridge St, Newcastle.
☎261 2526
Formerly Tiffanys, The Studio is aimed at the over-20s, and has a pub and a club. It's open five nights a week, from 9pm to 2am, with no membership requirement. Monday is student night: admission £1, with union card. On other nights you have to be smartly dressed (no jeans, trainers or t-shirts). Admission: Tues & Thurs, £1.50 before 11pm, £2 after; Fri & Sat, £3 before 11pm, £4 after.

TALK OF THE TYNE
Charles St, Gateshead. ☎478 1030
Formerly Bobby Pattinson's northern nightspot, now the talk of the over-30s, this is the place to *groove* to the disco sounds of yesteryear. Fri & Sat, £2 before 11pm, £2.50 after; Sun, £1.50 (inc. membership) before 9.30pm, 50p extra from 9.30 to 11pm (close). Monday is teenyboppers night (13-17 year olds); Tuesday singalong to the organ.

TUXEDO JUNCTION
Bamburgh House, Market St, Newcastle. ☎232 3211
The club is open to all members of the general public with no membership requirement. It's open Monday to Saturday from 8.30pm to 2am. The DJ plays a wide variety of music ranging from 50s jazz and alternative on Tuesday students night to the 60s and 70s music for over-25s on Wednesdays. Tuxedo's includes an à la carte restaurant and several bars. Another nightclub called **Manhattans** is linked to Tuxedo's, and is open from 6.30pm to 2am every night except Sunday, when the hours are 7–12pm, serving alcoholic drinks until 10.30pm then soft drinks afterwards.

WALKERS
Low Friar House, Blackfriars, Newcastle. ☎232 3303
Walkers is *the* dance club in the area, attracting the really smart set, with soul music and a hightech laser lightshow; the disco dancefloor and bar are upstairs. Admission varies from 20p to a maximum of £3 on Saturday nights. It's open all day from Monday to Saturday, from 11am till 2am the following morning, with the downstairs club café serving a wide range of food. On Friday and Saturday nights the café hosts the Dance Society; on Monday nights there's comedy in the café, with local acts plus jazz and swing bands, and during the Unhappy Hour they serve wrong-sized drinks till people get fed up. Westworld is the Wednesday student night, when jazz and blues bands play in the café, with admission free on showing a student union card.

ZOOTS
Waterloo St, Newcastle.
☎261 4507
A lively nightclub attracting all kinds of people. There's no membership, and no dress restrictions. Admission £2 on Friday and Saturday nights, when there's a live band, a comedian and disco from 7.30pm till 12.30am. The children's disco on Tuesdays is aimed at the 14 to 17 age group, with admission for £1. It's closed on other evenings. On Saturday afternoon there are exotic dancers, with free admission. Zoots is a popular venue for hen and stag parties.

Museums & Historic Buildings

NEWCASTLE

BESSIE SURTEES HOUSE
Sandhill, Quayside. ☎261 1136
Three architecturally priceless 16th and 17th century timber-framed houses which have recently been restored and now house the regional office of English Heritage. The main rooms are open to the public from 10am to 6pm each week day. Bessie Surtees, daughter of a rich Newcastle merchant, eloped to Scotland to marry John Scott, climbing out of one of the first floor windows. Scott became a respected lawyer, and later, as Lord Eldon, was Lord Chancellor of England.

BLACKFRIARS
Monk St, off Stowell St. ☎261 5367
Blackfriars is a 13th century Dominican friary later used by nine Craft Guilds. Now restored, it houses several craft workshops, the Blackfriars Brasserie (see Restaurants section), and the Tourist Centre with its exhibition of the history of Newcastle. Open daily, Easter–September, 10am–5pm; October–March, Tues–Sat, 10am–4.30pm.

CASTLE KEEP
Castle Garth, St Nicholas St, Newcastle. ☎232 7938
The keep was built by Henry II in 1172-77 on the site of the original New Castle, founded in 1080 by Robert Curthose, son of William the Conqueror. The city takes its name from it. The Black Gate on the other side of the railway is a medieval gatehouse to the castle, with 17th century houses built on top. The keep is open from 9.30am Tuesday to Sunday, till 5.30pm from April to September and till 4.30pm from October to March.

GREEK MUSEUM
Greek Museum, Percy Building, University. ☎232 8511
This museum in the University's Classics Department has a collection of Greek and Etruscan painted vases, terracotta and metalwork (including armour). The collection has a national reputation and is by far the most important of its kind in the North East. There is no admission charge and the museum is open on weekdays from 9.30am to 4.30pm during term time.

GREY'S MONUMENT
Grey St x Blackett St.
The monument was built in 1838 to commemorate the Reform Bill of 1832, championed by Earl Grey, one of the North East's greatest sons. As MP for Northumberland and later as Prime Minister, Grey fought for electoral reform and for the abolition of slavery. You can climb to the top of Grey's Monu-

ment on Saturdays and bank holidays (Easter to first Saturday in October), from 11.30am to 4.30pm. The view from the top over the city centre is breathtaking, but be warned: there are 164 steps!

HADRIAN'S WALL
Benwell and Denton.
Newcastle has two small Roman remains. The **Benwell Roman Temple** (off Broomridge Avenue) was dedicated to the local god Antenocitus, and has an apse at one end containing a statue base and flanked by altars. There is also a section of Hadrian's Wall at **Denton Hall Turret** next to the West Road at Denton Burn.

HANCOCK MUSEUM
Great North Rd x Claremont Rd.
☎222 7418
The only natural history museum in the region, with exhibits including two Egyptian mummies, a dodo and two great auks, as well as comprehensive collections of butterflies and birds. The Hancock displays used to consist largely of case after case of various stuffed creatures, but in recent years they have opened a Nature Shop and organised many of their exhibits into imaginative presentations featuring geology, birds, Thomas Bewick, the Hancock story, the rain forest, and the highly popular Abel's Ark. Northumbrian wildlife is well represented, and there are recorded birdsong commentaries including some mating calls. Open: Mon–Sat, 10am–5pm & Sundays, 2–5pm. Small admission charge.

JOICEY MUSEUM
John George Joicey Museum, City Rd. ☎232 4562
This "period" museum of old Newcastle is housed in the old Holy Jesus Hospital, a 17th century almshouse, with the 1880 General Soup Kitchen at one end. Displays include audio-visual presentations of the Great Fire of 1854 and the Tyne Flood of 1771 and period rooms from 17th to early 20th century. Also sporting guns from the North East and some regimental exhibits from the 15/19 King's Royal Hussars and the Northumberland Hussars. Open: Tues–Fri (+ bank holidays), 10am–5.30pm & Sat 10am–4.30pm. Free admission.

15/19 KING'S ROYAL HUSSARS REGIMENTAL MUSEUM
Fenham Barracks, Barrack Rd.
☎261 1046 x 3140.
Displays mainly of uniforms, weapons, medals, photographs, library documents, 1759 to present day. Because the museum is in the barracks, entry will depend upon the level of security in effect during opening hours. Usually open 9am–3pm, Mon–Fri, but ring before going to check. Closed weekends and bank holidays. Free admission.

● The Hancock Museum's Abel's Ark: the animals may be stuffed but they still go in two by two.

MILITARY VEHICLE MUSEUM
Exhibition Park Pavilion, Great North Rd. ☎281 7222
Private museum of jeeps, trucks, a tank and other vehicles which also has a large collection of other militaria including knives, daggers, bayonets, 25lb guns, searchlights, uniformed mannequins and bicycles. War films are shown in the video room. Open daily, 10am–4.30pm. Admission: adults £1, children 50p.

MUSEUM OF ANTIQUITIES
Quadrangle, University.
☎232 8511
The major museum of archaeology in North East England, from 6000 BC to AD 1600, with a renowned collection of artefacts, armour, models and diagrams relating to Hadrian's Wall. There are life-size figures of Roman soldiers and a reconstruction of a temple of Mithras. Open: Mon–Sat, 10am–5pm. Free admission.

MUSEUM OF SCIENCE & ENGINEERING
Blandford House, Blandford Sq.
☎232 6789
Industrial history museum with three major permanent displays on Motive Power, Ships and the Tyne, and Pioneers of Industry. There are many working models, and the most famous exhibit is the SS *Turbinia*, the world's first turbine-powered ship, surprise star-turn of the 1897 Spithead Review of the Fleet. The latest addition is Science Factory, with interactive "hands on" exhibits like lasers and a plasma globe. Open: Tues–Fri (+ bank holidays), 10am–5.30pm & Sat, 10am–4.30pm. Free admission.

NEWBURN HALL MOTOR MUSEUM
Townfield Gdns, Newburn.
☎264 2977
Veteran (pre-1920), vintage (1920-30) and post-vintage cars and motor cycles, including Grand Prix racers and famous cars from films and television – as seen in *Chariots of Fire* and *Brideshead Revisited*. Some cars are usually in the process of being restored, and all are on open display: they're meant to be examined at close quarters. Five miles from the city centre, off the A6085 (behind Newburn police station), the museum has a licensed bar and restaurant. Open: Tues–Sat (+ bank

holidays), 10am–9pm (last admission) & Sun, 10am–6pm; closed on Mondays but open on bank holidays. Admission: Adults £1.50, children 50p.

TRINITY MARITIME CENTRE
Broad Chare, Quayside.
☎261 4691
Old ship chandler's warehouse built in 1840 now a maritime museum with models of ships, nautical instruments, working models of marine and deck machinery. Models include the Quayside as it was in 1775 and ships built by Swan Hunters, including one of the RMS *Mauretania*. The Collingwood Room, with its display of shipping company flags, provides a suitable setting for many Quayside meetings. Open: Tues–Fri, 10.30am–4pm, April to September & 11am–3pm, October to March. Admission: Adults 50p, OAPs 30p, children 20p.

NORTHUMBERLAND

AYDON CASTLE
nr Corbridge. ☎043471-2450
Small 13th century fortified hall built as a manor house and later converted into a farmhouse in the 17th century. Open: Mon–Sat, 9.30am–6.30pm & Sun, 2–4pm. Closed in the winter.

BAGPIPE MUSEUM
The Chantry, Bridge St, Morpeth.
☎0670-519466
This unusual museum specialises in the history and development of Northumbrian small pipes and their music. They are set in the context of bagpipes around the world, from India to Inverness. An ingenious sound system brings the pipes to life: you can listen to the music through personal headphones and learn the difference between a rant and a reel. Open: Mon–Sat, 9.30am–5.30pm, March–December & 10am–4pm, January–February. Small admission charge.

BELSAY HALL
Belsay, Morpeth. ☎066181-636
Belsay Hall, Castle and Gardens: home of the Middleton family for 600 years, in 30 acres of landscaped gardens. The neoclassical hall was built in 1810-17 by Sir Charles Monck and the manor house adjoining the 14th century castle in 1614. Open: April–September, Mon–Sat, 9.30am–6.30pm & Sun, 11am–6.30pm; also winter weekends, 11am–4pm.

BLYTH TOWN MUSEUM
Croft Rd, Blyth. ☎0670-352116
Life in the Blyth Valley from late Victorian times. Will open for groups, day or evening by appointment. Open: April–June, Saturdays only, 11.30am–4pm; July–October, Tues & Sat, 11am–4pm.

CHANTRY MUSEUM
The Chantry, Bridge St, Morpeth.
☎0670-511323
The museum is in a 14th century Chantry also housing the Bagpipe Museum, the Northumbria Craft Centre and Tourist Information Centre. It's a small local museum of Northumberland life and environment, with exhibits including photographs, documents, posters and local Victorian artefacts. Open: Mon–Sat, 10am–5pm. Free admission.

HEXHAM ABBEY
Beaumont St, Hexham.
☎0434-602031
The abbey has a Saxon crypt, miseri-

cords, and 15th century paintings. It is a popular place for recitals and concerts, and the main venue in the summer for the Hexham Music Festival. Open daily from 9am, till 7pm from May to September and till 5pm during the winter months.

MIDDLE MARCH CENTRE FOR BORDER HISTORY
Manor Office, Hexham.
☎0434-604011
Border history museum specialising in 16th century, with armour, weapons, models of pele-houses and other fortified buildings, reconstructions of a smithy and a border home. Open: April–October, Mon–Fri, 10am–4.30pm; August weekends, 2–5pm.

SEATON DELAVAL HALL
Seaton Sluice. (Rt. Hon. Lord Hastings, ☎237 1493).
Magnificent house built for Admiral George Delaval by Sir John Vanbrugh in the Palladian style in 1718-29. Pevsner says of it: 'No other Vanbrugh house is so mature, so compact and so powerful, and the admiral, we know from one of Vanbrugh's letters, was "not disposed to starve the design at all".' The Hall's collection of period furniture, portraits and ceramics can be viewed – together with its stone stables – from May to September on Wednesdays, Sundays and bank holidays, 2–6pm.

JOHN SINCLAIR RAILWAY MUSEUM
Heatherslaw Mill, Ford & Etal Estate, Wooler. ☎089082-244
Local museum of the Blyth and Tyne Railway and other past northern railways, which now has its own light railway (four mile round trip). North of Wooler – signposted on the A697 – it's open from 10am to 6pm daily, admission free.

GEORGE STEPHENSON'S BIRTHPLACE
Wylam. ☎0661-853457
The inventor and engineer George Stephenson built the famous *Rocket* locomotive and constructed the first public railway, the Stockton to Darlington line. He was born in 1781 in this small small stone cottage, which dates from 1750. One room is open, with late 19th century furnishings. Open: April–October, Wed, Thurs, Sat, Sun, 2–5pm.

WALLINGTON HOUSE
Cambo, nr. Morpeth.
☎067-074 283
Built in 1688 on the site of an earlier medieval castle, Wallington is famous for its mid-18th century rococo interior and for its walled garden and grounds. The rooms include an early Georgian salon and a Victorian nursery; there is a collection of dolls' houses and in the coachhouse a display of old coaches. It also has a restaurant. Open: 1–5.30pm, April–September, daily except Tues; October, Wed, Sat, Sun. The grounds are open all year and the walled garden daily April–September, 10am–7pm; October, 10am–6pm; November–March, 10am–4pm.

WOODHORN CHURCH MUSEUM
Woodhorn Village, Ashington.
☎0670-817371
A Saxon church with medieval bells and a carved 17th century wooden chair. It has a craft centre and picnic area, and puts on concerts and other activities. Open all year: Wed–Sun (+ bank holidays), 10am–12.30pm & 1–4pm.

WOODHORN COLLIERY MUSEUM
Woodhorn, Ashington.
☎0670-856968
New museum of Northumberland coal-mining, not yet complete.

WYLAM RAILWAY MUSEUM
Falcon Centre, Falcon Tce, Wylam.
☎0661 852174

Displays show the importance of Wylam in the history of the railways, featuring the work of famous Wylam railway pioneers George Stephenson, Timothy Hackworth, William Hedley and Nicholas Wood. Open: Tues, Thurs, 2–5pm & 5.30–7.30pm; Sat, 9–12am.

NORTH TYNESIDE

ST MARY'S LIGHTHOUSE
Bait Island, Whitley Bay.
☎252 0853
Three buildings are open to the public: the lighthouse itself, the keeper's cottage and a birdwatching cottage. Opening times depend on the tides.

STEPHENSON RAILWAY MUSEUM
Middle Engine Lane, North Shields.
☎262 2627
This expanding collection of steam locomotives and vintage rail carriages features the original Stephenson *Killingworth Billy*, one of the earliest steam locomotives in the world. Situated at the junction of several former colliery waggonways, the Stephenson Railway Museum Project is to have steam trains running along the old line from near the Percy Main metro station offering visitors an exciting way of getting to the museum. It forms part of the Stephenson Project which also takes in **Dial Cottage** on Great Lime Road, Killingworth, where George and his son Robert Stephenson lived when they were developing their first locomotives.

TYNEMOUTH PRIORY & CASTLE
Tynemouth. ☎257 1090.
Built over a 7th century monastery, the priory was the burial place of ancient Northumbrian kings until the Vikings destroyed it. Today the churchyard contains the graves of many mariners whose headstones face the sea. The 14th century castle with its massive gatehouse was built to defend the priory, and was later used to guard the entrance to the River Tyne. On view are powder magazines used during the First and Second World Wars for coastal defence, and a cannon commemorating the Tynemouth Volunteer Artillery, the British Army's first volunteer gunners. Open: April–September, Mon–Sat, 9.30am–6.30pm; Sun, 2–6.30pm; October–March, Mon–Sat, 9.30am–4pm; Sun, 2–4pm.

TYNEMOUTH VOLUNTEER LIFE BRIGADE
Spanish Battery, nr Collingwood Monument, Tynemouth.
☎257 2059
The Tynemouth brigade was formed to help mariners wrecked on the Black Midden rocks in the Tyne estuary, the first ship-to-shore rescue service in the world. This museum of maritime history in the brigade's watchhouse (1887) includes relics from ships wrecked at Tynemouth since 1864, as well as paintings, models, ship figureheads and rescue equipment. Car parking nearby. Open: Tues–Sat, 10am–

3pm; Sun, 10–12am. Admission free.

ADMIRAL COLLINGWOOD MONUMENT
Tynemouth.
Collingwood is one of Tyneside's famous sons: he went to sea at the age of 11, and later, in 1805, as second-in-command of the British fleet, won the Battle of Trafalgar as Nelson lay dying from his wounds. The Collingwood Monument, one of three around the country, was built in 1845. Below it are four guns from his ship the *Royal Sovereign*, the only surviving guns of their type apart from the *Victory*'s.

WALLSEND HERITAGE CENTRE
Buddle St, Wallsend. ☎262 0012
Just north of the Segedunum Fort excavations, the centre specialises in Roman archaeology, local, social and industrial history, and houses Roman relics from the digs as well as a scaled-down model of the *Mauretania*, the world's largest liner when launched from Wallsend in 1906. The wide range of exhibits including the famous *Portable Shrine to Mercury* display. Open: Tues–Fri, 10am–5.30pm; Sat, 10am–4.30pm; Sun, 2–5pm. Admission free. Car parking and facilities for disabled visitors.

——————SOUTH OF THE TYNE——————

ARBEIA ROMAN FORT
Baring St, South Shields.
☎456 1369
Overlooking the mouth of the Tyne, the fort was built at about the same time as Hadrian's Wall. The West Gate has been reconstructed using authentic materials, with the fittings copying Roman originals but in such a way as to allow public access to displays including a quartermaster's store, replica Roman military equipment and a scale model of the fort. Open: Easter–September, Tues–Fri, 10am–5.30pm; Sat, 10am–4.30pm; Sun, 2–5pm; open on bank holidays but closed on Sundays and from October to Easter.

BEDE GALLERY
Springwell Park, Butchersbridge, Jarrow. ☎489 1807
Little museum of Jarrow's political, social and industrial history, coupled with an art gallery. Displays cover the Jarrow March, Palmers Yard and the gibbeting of William Jobling, and include an Jarrow March banner and a Laurie Wheatley sculpture of William Jobling hanging from the original gibbet. Open: Tues–Fri, 10am–5pm; Sun, 2–5pm; Sat, Mon, closed.

BEDE MONASTERY MUSEUM
Jarrow Hall, Church Bank, Jarrow.
☎489 2106
A small museum which has as its permanent collection much of the excavated material from the nearby **St Paul's Monastery**, home of the Venerable Bede, including a Saxon window and a model of the monastery, which was built in 682. Not much of the monastery itself is left: there are some remains of cloister buildings, and part of Bede's church has survived in the chancel of St

PLACES TO SEE   117

Paul's Church, which still has its dedication stone dated 23 April AD 685. The café is open for morning coffee, lunch and afternoon tea. The museum is open April to October, Tues–Sat, 10am–5.30pm; Sun, 2.30–5.30pm; November to March, Tues–Sun, 2.30–5.30pm. Admission: Adults 60p, children, OAPs 30p.

BEWICK BIRTHPLACE MUSEUM
Cherryburn, Mickley, nr Stocksfield. ☎0661-843276
Wood engraver and naturalist Thomas Bewick (1753-1828) was Northumbria's greatest artist – who worked on the smallest scale. Situated on the south bank of the Tyne 12 miles west of Newcastle, the museum includes the cottage where Bewick was born as well as a farmyard and animals. The exhibition of Bewick's work features his engravings for animal, bird and children's books of 200 years ago. There is a printing house where you can see Bewick engravings being printed from his original woodblocks. The bookshop has genuine Bewick prints for sale. Open: Tues–Sun (+ bank holidays), 10am–5pm. Admission: Adults £1.50 per adult with reductions for students and OAPs.

BOWES RAILWAY
Springwell Village, nr Wrekenton. ☎416 1847
Bowes is the world's only preserved standard gauge rope-hauled railway, designed by George Stephenson and opened in 1826. Originally 15 miles long, the railway carried coal from several collieries to the Tyne at Jarrow. Now run by volunteers, it has steam-hauled passenger trains which will take you from Springwell up the incline to the steam-driven engine house at Blackham's Hill, and there are tours of the locomotive sheds and workshops. Open most Sundays and bank holidays from late March to early September, from 10am, with trains running from 12am to 5pm. Admission: Adults £1.50, children, OAPs, 75p.

GIBSIDE CHAPEL
Gibside, Burnopfield.
☎0207-542255
This was a mausoleum for five members of the Bowes family built to a design by James Payne between 1760 and 1812 and restored in 1965. It is an outstanding example of Palladian church architecture; there is a rare mahogany three-tier decker pulpit and boy pews in cherrywood. It also has an avenue of turkey oaks and a woodland walk, plus a picnic area, shop and tea room. Open: March–October, Wed, Sat, Sun (+ bank holidays), 1–5pm. Admission: Adults £1, children 50p.

PENSHAW MONUMENT
Penshaw Hill.
In the famous local legend of the Lambton Worm, the giant dragon wrapped itself around Penshaw Hill, a prominent landmark between Washington and Sunderland visible for miles around. The monument on the top is a memorial to John Lambton, first Earl of Durham, who was the first Governor of Canada. Based on the design of the Temple of Theseus in Athens (only half the size), it was erected by public subscription in 1844.

PRUDHOE CASTLE
Prudhoe. ☎0661-33459
Ruined 12th century castle overlooking the Tyne, once owned by the Percy family. The keep and gatehouse are among the oldest in Britain. Open: April–September, daily, 9.30am–6.30pm; October–March,

Mon, Tues, Fri (alternate), Sat, 9.30am–4pm & Sun, 2–4pm.

SOUTH SHIELDS MUSEUM
Ocean Rd, South Shields.
☎456 8740
The recently enlarged and improved museum shows the archaeology, geology, industrial and social history of the South Shields area, with displays featuring local shipbuilding and the lifeboat, natural history and transport. The Catherine Cookson gallery portrays life on Tyneside where she grew up, using photographs and street re-constructions. Exhibits include the original printing press of the South Shields Gazette from 1855. An art gallery and a tourist information centre are also housed in the museum. Open: Tues–Fri, 10am–5.30pm; Sat, 10am–4.30pm; Sun, 2–5pm; plus bank holidays. Admission free.

TANFIELD RAILWAY
Marley Hill, Sunniside.
Opened in 1725, this is the oldest existing railway in the world. Originally a colliery line which took coal from several collieries for loading onto ships at Dunston Staithes, it was eventually taken over by North Eastern Railways, and finally closed by British Railways in 1964. The Tanfield Railway Company now has over 30 steam locomotives, and operates a passenger service from the shed at Sunniside, where there is a restored workshop, an exhibition centre and a rare collection of pre-1900 railway carriages. Open: daily, 10am–4pm, longer at weekends.

WASHINGTON 'F' PIT MUSEUM
Albany Way, District 2, Washington. ☎416 7640
The 'F' Pit Museum is a monument to 250 years of coal mining in the North East. It houses a Victorian steam winding engine, the last one in the Durham and Northumberland coalfield. Built in 1888, it is an outstanding example of 19th century engineering and was capable of lifting 120 tons of coal an hour from a seam 712 feet underground. The engine worked until the pit closed, but the pithead gear is now turned by an electric motor for demonstration purposes. Open: April–October, Tues–Fri (+ bank holidays), 10am–5.30pm; Sat, 10am–4.30pm; Sun, 2–5pm; closed lunchtimes, 1–1.30pm, and from November to March. Admission free. Car parking.

WASHINGTON OLD HALL
The Avenue, District 4, Washington. ☎416 6879
This was the ancestral home of the George Washington's ancestors, from 1183 to 1613. Exhibits include 17th century furniture, oil paintings, Delft etc. There are also documents signed by George Washington. American Independence celebrations are held here each 4th of July, and President Jimmy Carter paid a famous visit to the Hall to plant a tree – which later died. Open: 11am–5pm; April, Wed, Sat, Sun; May–September, daily except Fridays. Admission: Adults £1, children 50p. Car parking.

7 Days out from Tyneside

BEAMISH MUSEUM
Beamish Hall, nr Stanley.
☎0207 231811
The North of England Open Air Museum at Beamish probably has more of old Tyneside on show than Tyneside itself does today. Buildings from throughout the region have been taken down brick by brick and then rebuilt at Beamish and furnished to show how the people of the North of England lived and worked early this century. There are four main areas: an old town street, a working farm, a colliery community and the railway station. Beamish was voted European Museum of the Year 1987 and British Museum of the Year 1986. Allow at least four hours for your visit. Open: April–October, daily, 10am–6pm; November–March, Tues–Sun, 10am–5pm. Admission: Summer, adults £4.50, children & OAPs, £3.50; winter, adults £2.50, children & OAPs £1.50. Free car parking.

CRAGSIDE HOUSE
Rothbury. ☎0669-20333
Set in 900 acres of country park with its many varieties of trees and rhododendrons, this Victorian Mansion House was the home of Tyneside

● Take a ride down Memory Lane at Beamish Museum.

120   PLACES TO SEE

industrialist and inventor Lord Armstrong. The original interior and furniture were largely designed by Norman Shaw, and the house also has Armstrong's collection of Pre-Raphaelite paintings. It was the first house to be lit by electricity generated from water power. Go on the Power Circuit, a two-mile walk taking in Armstrong's hydraulic and hydroelectric machinery, including his hydraulic lift and kitchen spit. Open: 1–5.30pm, April–September, Tues–Sun (+ bank holidays); October, Wed, Sat & Sun. The park is open off season, but not the house. Admission: Adults £3, children £1.50.

DURHAM CATHEDRAL
Durham. ☎386 2367
Durham Cathedral is the finest example of Norman church architecture in Britain, a magnificent cathedral built in the form of a Latin cross. Alec-Clifton Taylor describes it thus: 'With the Cathedral of Durham we reach the incomparable masterpiece of Romanesque architecture not only in England but anywhere. The moment of entering provides for an architectural experience never to be forgotten: one of the greatest that England has to offer.' Work on the building started in 1093, with additions made till about 1500. Here lie St Cuthbert's remains, brought by the wandering monks from Lindisfarne, as well as Bede's tomb. Durham Cathedral is open all year round. **Durham Castle** on nearby Palace Green was founded in 1072. Formerly the seat of the Bishops of Durham, it now forms part of Durham University; the kitchens date from 1499, and the Great Hall from 1284.

HADRIAN'S WALL
The Roman Wall was 80 miles long, stretching from the Solway Firth to Wallsend. Started in AD 122, it was built on the orders of Emperor Hadrian 'to separate the Romans from the Barbarians' – the warring Picts to the north. The best parts can be seen to the west in Northumberland and Cumbria. However, there are some substantial remains between Newcastle and the North Tyne, with a fine 280-yard stretch at **Heddon-on-the-Wall**. Corbridge was once the prosperous Roman town of Corstopitum, and there are extensive remains at the **Corbridge Roman Museum** (☎043-471 2349). Hadrian's Wall crossed the North Tyne at Chollerford where the **Chesters Roman Fort** (☎043481-379), built for 500 cavalrymen, has the finest military bath-house in Britain as well as barrack blocks and gateways. Nearby is the site of the Battle of Heavenfield, where Northumbria's Christian king Oswald defeated the heathen British in 634. West of the North Tyne the best Roman sites are: **Housesteads Roman Fort** (☎04984-363); the **Vindolanda Museum** (☎04984 277) at Chesterholm, near Bardon Mill; and the **Roman Army Museum** (☎06972-485) at Carvoran, Greenhead, and the nearby **Walltown Crags** wall and turret.

KIELDER
Kielder Water is the largest manmade lake in Europe, a vast reservoir surrounded by the Kielder Forest created by the flooding of the North Tyne. To the north are the Cheviots and the Scottish border country, to the south Wark Forest and the North Pennines. There are information centres at either end of the lake. The **Kielder Water Visitor Centre** (☎0660-40398) at Tower Knowe, Falstone, has displays showing the construction of the Kielder Water Scheme, and at Leaplish a waterside park with water sports, fishing, log

cabins and a caravan site. It's open from 10am till 6pm from April to September and till 4pm for the rest of the year (but is closed at Christmas and New Year). At the other end of Kielder Water, just inside the Scottish border, **Kielder Castle** has a Forestry Commission information centre (☎0660-50209) with graphic displays on forestry and the local and natural history of the area. This is open from 10am till 6pm from April to October and from 10.30am till 4pm during the winter months.

LINDISFARNE
Holy Island, Northumberland
Founded by St Aidan, **Lindisfarne** was the birthplace of Christianity in northern Europe, and home of the beautifully illustrated Lindisfarne Gospels. The first monastery was built by the monks from Iona in 635 and Cuthbert became bishop 50 years later. When Lindsfarne was sacked by the Danes in 875, the monks began their years of wandering with the precious relics of St Cuthbert (said to have miraculous healing properties), finally burying his remains at Durham.

Lindisfarne Priory (☎0289-89200) dates from 1090, when Benedictine monks returned to the island, and the priory museum contains stones from the Anglian and Viking periods, a collection of medieval pottery, and reproductions of the Lindisfarne Gospels (now in the British Museum). During the summer months of April to September the priory and museum are open daily from 9.30am to 6.30pm, and the nearby Lindsfarne mead factory is also open to the public.

Lindisfarne Castle (☎0289-89244) is a fort built about 1550, and converted into a private house in 1903 by Sir Edwin Lutyens. It has 17th century Flemish and English oak furniture as well as some contemporary pieces designed by Lutyens, and the beautiful garden was landscaped by Gertrude Jekyll. Open: April–September, 11am–5pm (except Friday but open on Good Friday); October, Sat & Sun, 11am–5pm (last admission 4.30pm). If you're driving up to Holy Island from Tyneside, check the tide times first (ring Newcastle City Information Service at the Central Library, ☎261 0691): you can only cross the causeway to Holy Island at low tide, and the island is cut off for several hours every day. You can always plan your trip to take in one of the Northumberland castles on the way: **Warkworth Castle** (☎0665-711423), seat of the Percy family, with its magnificent 15th century keep; **Alnwick Castle** (☎0665-510777), home of the Duke of Northumberland; **Dunstanburgh Castle** (☎066576-231) at Craster; and **Bamburgh Castle** (☎06684-208), just south of Lindisfarne.

From Lindisfarne you can also see the **Farne Islands**, now a nature reserve with a large colony of grey seals and many different kinds of seabirds. There are boat trips from Seahouses to Inner Farne and Staple Island or around the islands at various times during the summer; ring the National Trust for details (☎0665-721099).

WILDFOWL & WETLANDS CENTRE, WASHINGTON
District 15, Washington.
☎416 5454
The best wildfowl park in the North of England, the home of over 1000 birds of over 100 varieties, including five of the rarest birds in the world: the white-winged wood duck, white-headed duck, Hawaiian goose, Philippine duck and New Zealand brown teal. The wetlands centre has one of only two flocks of captive-bred flamingoes, which are named after characters from Catherine Cookson novels. There are also many wild birds, mammals and plants, and facilities include a viewing gallery, picnic areas, various hides and a winter wildbird feeding station. Open: daily, 9.30am–5pm.

ART GALLERIES

BEDE GALLERY
Springwell Park, Butchersbridge, Jarrow. ☎489 1807
Art gallery coupled with a museum of Jarrow's political, social and industrial history (see Museums section). The gallery has a varied programme of contemporary art exhibitions and events, and also hosts regular touring exhibitions. Permanent exhibits include a Laurie Wheatley sculpture of William Jobling hanging from the infamous Jarrow Slake gibbet. Open: Tues–Fri, 10am–5pm; Sun, 2–5pm; Sat, Mon, closed. Admission free.

CHARLOTTE PRESS
Charlotte Sq, Newcastle.
☎232 7531
Charlotte Press is a printmakers' workshop which displays and sells work by member artists as well as prints taken from Thomas Bewick's original blocks. It is a rare centre of artistic excellence used by some of the best contemporary artists in the the north of England, and most of the work on show is good quality, unpretentious and not too expensive; the displays are changed every month. If you want to try printmaking yourself, Charlotte Press also runs courses on etching, screenprinting, metal plate and stone lithography, and it has a membership scheme for artists who want to use its facilities. Open: 10am–6pm. Admission free. Parking restricted to nearby car parks and metered streets.

HATTON GALLERY
Quadrangle, Newcastle University.
☎232 8511
Attached to the Fine Art Department of the University, the Gallery is noted for hosting a wide variety of art exhibitions, many of both local and international significance. One permanent exhibit is the Elterwater Merzbarn by Dadaist artist Kurt

ARTS 123

Schwitters, a large part-painted sculpture constructed in the end wall of a Lake District barn during the 1940s when Schwitters was living in exile in Britain. The Hatton also has a portrait of Schwitters by his friend Fred Uhlman as well as Uhlman's collection of African sculpture. When exhibitions are on, the gallery is open weekdays 10am–5pm and Saturdays in term time 10am–4.30pm; closed on Sundays and in vacation time on Saturdays. Admission free.

LAING ART GALLERY
Higham Place, Newcastle.
☎232 7734
Opened in 1904, the Laing has the biggest collection of art treasures in the North East, including paintings, watercolours, costume, silver, glass and pottery. It changes its own displays and is a major regional centre for touring exhibitions. Special features of the collections include Gauguin's *The Breton Shepherdess*, the spectacular paintings of the great northern Romantic artist John Martin, and the beautiful 18th century glass enamelled by William Beilby of Newcastle. Displays of oil paintings and sculpture include the elegant 18th century *Portrait of Mrs Riddell* by Reynolds, the 19th century opulence of three large canvasses by Landseer, Burne-Jones's brilliant *Laus Veneris*, and the work of more modern British artists such as Stanley Spencer, Lucian Freud and Henry Moore. Open: Tues–Fri, 10am–5.30pm; Sat, 10am–4.30pm; Sun, 2–5pm; closed Mondays but open on bank holidays. There is access for wheelchairs through a separate entrance with doorbell, but groups of disabled people are advised to telephone beforehand. Admission free.

POLYTECHNIC GALLERY
Sandyford Rd, Newcastle.
☎232 6002
The Polytechnic Gallery is above the Polytechnic Library, opposite the Civic Centre, and runs an imaginative programme of international exhibitions, usually of 20th century art, as well as showing the work of northern artists, including the annual Polytechnic fine art degree show. It has built up a special relationship with the Munch Museum in Oslo, and several major Edvard Munch exhibitions have come to Newcastle direct from Norway before being toured around Britain and Europe. Open from 10am, Mon–Thurs till 6pm, Fri–Sat till 4pm. Admission free.

SHIPLEY ART GALLERY
Prince Consort Rd, Gateshead.
☎477 1495
Opened in 1917 to display part of the large collection of British and Old Master paintings bequeathed to

Gateshead by Joseph Shipley, the gallery has major works by Tintoretto (*Christ Washing the Disciples' Feet*), David Teniers the Younger, Benjamin Cuyp and other Dutch and Flemish painters. As well as showing changing exhibitions of local and national importance and selections from the decorative art and local history collections, the gallery now specialises in traditional and contemporary British craft. It has on permanent display the most comprehensive collection of contemporary craft in the North of England, and also runs a series of craft classes, workshops, lectures and demonstrations throughout the year. Open: Tues–Fri, 10am–5.30pm; Sat, 10am–4.30pm; Sun, 2–5pm; closed on Mondays but open on bank holidays. Admission free.

SIDE GALLERY
Side, Quayside, Newcastle.
☎232 2208
Side Gallery is a photographic gallery with two exhibition spaces showing regional, national and international photography within a broadly based documentary tradition. It aims to respond to and promote photography of the highest standard with a special commitment to the northern region. It also has a study centre which provides a reference source of a wide range of published material on film and photography. Books, posters, videos, postcards and publications are on sale in the bookshop. Open: Tues–Sun, 11am–5pm; closed on Mondays. Admission free.

ARTS CENTRES

BUDDLE ARTS CENTRE
Station Road, Wallsend.
☎262 4276
A thriving community-based arts centre which is well supported by local people. As well as staging plays, puppet shows and musical events, the Buddle organises various kinds of workshops and puts on exhibitions, mainly by local artists and photographers. Open: Tues–Fri, 10am–9pm; Sat, 10am–1pm, 2–5pm, 6–9pm; plus evening events with licensed bar; closed Sundays, Mondays, and first two weeks in September.

DANCE CITY
Peel Lane, off Waterloo St, Newcastle. ☎261 0505
The home of English New Dance Theatre, Dance City runs an energetic programme of classes, workouts and workshops on all kinds and aspects of dance at all levels. This run-through of some of their activities shows something of their range: movement technique, ballet, workout, children's tap, jazz, stretch 'n' relax (with creche), creative, tai chi, etc. There are regular specialist workshops for more advanced dancers with an emphasis on multicultural dance forms, and for the real aficionados a week-long summer school. Dance City is open from 9am, but classes don't start until midday. Most classes and workouts are at lunchtimes, in the evening or on Saturday mornings, and prices range from 75p to £2.60 (plus concessions). There is also an all-day vegetarian café (see entry in Restaurants section). English New Dance Theatre is an internationally renowned company which performs all over the country and abroad, and Jacky Lansley is artistic director of ENDT and Dance City.

LITERARY & PHILOSOPHICAL SOCIETY
Lower Westgate Rd, Newcastle.
☎232 0192
The Lit & Phil is not an arts centre in the modern sense, but it has been fulfilling a similar function in Newcastle since 1793, when it was founded by William Turner and a group of radicals and scientists as a debating society. Housed near the Central Station in a magnificent Doric pillared and portalled building (built in 1822-5 by John Green), it has one of the few private subscription libraries in the country, with over 100,000 books, manuscripts and records. The atmosphere is rather hushed and scholarly, but it's also a friendly place where you can have a cup of coffee while leafing through some of the latest magazines. It may seem a little old-fashioned, but it's also a sanctuary from the money-grabbing world

outside, a civilising place which still upholds the importance of the arts and sciences in our impoverished culture. You can actually take out some of the dusty leather-bound antique tomes, along with the latest novels or CDs from the comprehensive classical music section. The building also has a warren of other rooms used for talks and meetings and for lunchtime and evening chamber music concerts and recitals. Here it was that Joseph Swan gave the first public demonstration of the incandescent electric lamp (forerunner of our light bulb), in 1879. Bodies who use the Lit & Phil today range from the Tyneside Humanist Society and the Workers' Educational Association to the Northumbrian Pipers' Society and the North East England Alpine and Rock Garden Group. An annual subscription to the Literary & Philosophical Society will cost you £34 (students and under-30s £17, families £50).

NEWCASTLE ARTS CENTRE
Lower Westgate Rd, Newcastle. ☎261 5618
Newcastle Arts Centre runs arts courses and events, and has its own studio theatre, exhibition basement, and two shops, Details, the best stocked shop for artists' materials in Newcastle, and the Frameshop. The shop is open all week, and the exhibition centre from 9.30am to 5pm during exhibitions. Also housed in the Arts Centre complex are Projects UK (see below), Folkworks (an agency for traditional music and dance), several artists' studios, the Rendezvous French bistro, Des's Drum Pad (a specialist music shop), the Beanpot wholefood shop, and a National Trust shop and information centre.

PROJECTS UK
Black Swan Court, Lower Westgate Rd, Newcastle. ☎232 2410
What is Projects UK?... 'An Art and Media Resource Centre initiating new and innovative work in arts and media with two hardware bases – Photography and Audio. Projects UK has a continuing programme of events, courses, concerts, festivals, etc, most taking place outside the Centre in site specific installations and exhibitions.' Among its facilities are sound studios equipped with the latest audio technology, fully equipped high-tech darkrooms, and the most comprehensive archive of performance art in Britain. The office is open 9.30am–5.30pm, Mon–Sat, and the studios Wed–Sat, 10am–5.30pm and on Thursdays till 9.30pm.

WASHINGTON ARTS CENTRE
Biddick Farm, Fatfield, District 7, Washington. ☎417 6213
Also known as North Biddick Farm Art Centre. Its exhibitions of paintings in the main bar and the granary bar change once a month, and are open to the public. There is a full, wide ranging programme of courses and classes on everything from poetry to pottery. The many events include tea dances, rock nights (with live bands), piano recitals, folk, jazz and cabaret nights and art marts. From September to April there are puppet shows for the kids, and the Washington Theatre Group stage two shows a year in the studio theatre, which is a regular venue for fringe theatre groups and other small theatre companies. It's not an easy place to find amidst the maze of Washington New Town's roundabouts and flyovers, but follow signs for District 7 and you'll end up there without knowing how. Open: Tues–Sat, 10am–5pm; plus some evenings for particular events.

THEATRE

Theatre on Tyneside offers two extremes of excellence. The biggest draw is the annual four to six-week Royal Shakespeare Company season: major plays and studio productions have been staged in Newcastle theatres and other Tyneside venues every year since 1976, with the RSC programme now centred on the Theatre Royal. At the other end of the scale is the Live Theatre Co: skilful innovators in community theatre and champions of new and native writing, who have taken theatre back to its roots, playing to every kind of audience, from striking miners to schoolchildren.

Between these two, there is an enormous variety of drama on offer, some of it as good or better than anything you'll find in London, and some of it...well, not so good. Publicity leaflets on the latest productions are always spread around the city – in places like the Central Library, the Tyneside Cinema and the Theatre Royal box office – and sometimes you can pick up a copy of one of the free listings magazines, which appear at the end of the month to publicise the next month's shows but disappear before you've had time to think about what you want to see.

The following sketches on performing arts venues tell you what you can expect from each venue. As well as the main venues in Newcastle, others are included not just on Tyneside but throughout the North East. It must say something about the quality of theatre in the region that people will come from as far afield as North Yorkshire or the Scottish borders to go to a play in Newcastle, and that when word gets round, Tynesiders will go to Durham, Hexham, Washington or even Sunderland to see the current *buzz* play which everyone is talking about.

THEATRE ROYAL
Grey St, Newcastle. ☎232 2061
An integral feature of the magnificent Grey Street architecture, the Theatre Royal is the region's premier theatrical venue. It underwent a major refurbishment, courtesy of Newcastle City Council and the EEC in 1987 and re-opened to a fanfare of publicity and civic pride. The theatre seems to attract controversy. On re-opening, much public debate surrounded the ceiling painting in the foyer by a local transvestite artist, Stephen Rowe. The press worried that the adventurous work was too risqué for such prestigious surrounds. The artist worried that he only finished the job two hours before the official opening.

Further controversy surrounds the theatre's funding. Newcastle City Council invests enormous sums in the building, leading to two recurring problems: that the theatre must always be full, and that the product is suitable for the city ratepayers, as well as the well-to-do's from outside the boundaries. The highlight of the Royal's year is the annual spring visit of the Royal Shakespeare Company. The RSC's programme appears to have diminished in recent years but no one doubts their commitment to the city. Indeed the theatre's refurbishment was apparently as a result of the RSC's complaints at backstage conditions.

For the rest of the year, the Royal is a number one receiving venue: anything from Roland Rat and popular panto stars, to Scottish Opera and pre- and post-West End shows, an impressive range for a 1200-seat theatre under pressure to fill every seat. Book balancing is supported by an attractive series of bars, restaurants and bistros around the theatre itself.

SUNDERLAND EMPIRE
High St West, Sunderland.
☎514 2517

The area's second largest theatre is also the subject of much civic pride, an imposing building in downtown Sunderland but a venue which struggles to impose itself on Wearside. Its "White Elephant" tag is far from the truth. The Empire is under less political pressure than its Tyneside counterpart and its artistic programme is notably more adventurous. It also attracts tours with television stars, but boasts regular visits from Sadlers Wells, interesting theatre and dance troupes from overseas, and quality jazz presentations. The Empire's pantomime is often as star-laden as the Theatre Royal's offering.

TYNE THEATRE & OPERA HOUSE
Westgate Rd, Newcastle.
☎232 0899.

Another recently refurbished Victorian theatre in Newcastle, the Tyne dates from 1867. A quite beautiful theatre, it was lovingly restored by a dedicated group of amateurs who own the building, with support from the public purse. Its rich history is told in the foyers of the building, and the tales of fire, closure and renewal are almost worth a visit in their own right. The Tyne recently played host to the **Tyne Theatre Company**, the region's leading repertory company and a beneficiary of Arts Council funding. But an unsuccessful year, followed by acrimonious arguments between the two very different organisations, led to the amateurs politely requesting the professional tenants to leave the building. Despite pressure from London, the city fathers, and an assortment of the great and the good, no compromise could be reached. The old theatre will continue to present successful amateur plays and musicals, as well as a series of bought-in shows. And another episode will pass into the theatre's controversial history.

The Tyne Theatre Company, having found itself new headquarters, will continue to produce a range of work in venues as diverse as the Theatre Royal, the Playhouse and Live Theatre. They tend to concentrate on new productions of classic texts, but given the new situation, a wide range of productions is expected.

NEWCASTLE PLAYHOUSE
Barras Bridge, Newcastle.
☎232 7079
The Playhouse nextdoor to the University is a rather strange venue. It is a commercially run theatre, one of the few outside London. It attempts to make money in a variety of ways: a lively bar and foyer host live music, mostly jazz and blues, most days; a food bar attracts shoppers and students alike. The main theatre hosts visits from medium size touring theatre companies and home grown entertainments, also a diverse and hard to classify range of musicians. Tom Robinson, Abdullah Ibrahim and Chris Barber have been three popular visitors. The Playhouse occasionally holds high quality late night cabaret sessions.

GULBENKIAN STUDIO
Gulbenkian Studio, Kings Walk, Newcastle. ☎232 9974
Adjacent to the Playhouse is the Gulbenkian, a studio theatre owned by Newcastle University. It is an excellent small space and the primary venue for small scale touring theatre companies and the RSC's studio work. The Gulbenkian regularly welcomes the likes of Joint Stock, Paines Plough and Tara Arts.

LIVE THEATRE
Broad Chare, Newcastle.
☎261 2694
The only venue on Newcastle's increasingly fashionable Quayside. Sited in a converted 18th century warehouse, this 100-seat cabaret-style venue is home to the area's oldest theatre company, Live Theatre Co. The company is the only one in the region dedicated to new writing and has established relationships with local talents like Tom Hadaway and the late C.P. Taylor, as well as national names like Alan Plater and Graham Reid. The plays are toured around the North but have extended runs in this Quayside home. The venue side of the operation is poorly funded, so Live Theatre hosts visiting companies on an irregular basis, mostly fellow new writing companies. It also gives local youth and community groups the chance to perform in a professional theatre space.

CAEDMON HALL
Prince Consort Rd, Gateshead.
☎477 3478
Gateshead's municipally run venue in the central library complex is an increasingly well used theatre, relating well to larger events in the leisure centre nextdoor. The Council has an interesting booking policy, taking visiting theatre companies from inside and outside the northern region, initiating festival events of its own, and showcasing music of all kinds. It is not a venue much loved by performers, but offers consistent artistic challenges to its neighbours over the Tyne Bridge.

BUDDLE ARTS CENTRE
Station Rd, Wallsend. ☎262 4276
Wallsend's arts centre is well worth the trip to this traditionally industrial area. The centre is again a hybrid of theatre, music and community events, very much a centre for all art forms. It is a community resource holding, with regular workshops, evening classes and discussion groups for local people. The Buddle future is often subject to uncertainty due to its unfashionable surrounds, but it remains a well used local centre for the arts, encouraging spectating and participating alike.

BEDE TOWER
Sunderland Polytechnic, Burdon Rd. ☎567 6191
The Bede is a small theatre run by Sunderland Polytechnic. It mainly

DRAMATIC OPPOSITES: Donald McBride *(left)* prepares to shave a corpse in Live Theatre's *In Blackberry Time*, adapted by Alan Plater and Michael Chaplin from the stories of Tyneside novelist Sid Chaplin; the Royal Shakespeare Company's Anton Lesser *(right)* playing Richard III at the Theatre Royal.

hosts visits from local touring companies such as Live Theatre Co, and is an alternative to the much larger Empire. The Bede Tower also hosts a wide variety of excellent student events.

WASHINGTON ARTS CENTRE
Biddick Farm, Fatfield, District 7, Washington. ☎416 6440
Situated in the unpleasant Biddick Farm area of Washington New Town, this arts centre performs a similar role to the Buddle in Wallsend and is perhaps a slightly more exciting centre. Washington is not an area associated with the arts but the Centre is attracting renewed interest with a lively mix of local and incoming attractions, from theatre to dance and even cabaret. Far more adventurous than the Bede Tower, Washington Arts Centre is probably the best bet for a challenging night out on Wearside.

AMATEUR THEATRE
As well as the group at the Tyne, the area boasts an array of amateur dramatic companies, many of which have their own theatres. The oldest, and best known, is the **Peoples Theatre** in Stephenson Road, Heaton (☎265 5020). The Peoples had radical beginnings in the early part of the century, offering opportunities for working men and women to take part in theatrical productions. In this they were supported by well-known figures including George Bernard Shaw. Today, the Peoples is noted for its highly adventurous programme and its array of activities, from full-length plays to studio productions, exhibitions, concerts, and a youth theatre. The Peoples may have moved away from its radical origins, but its spirit and range of work is a lesson to its professional neighbours. In recent years the RSC have

ARTS   **131**

played at the Peoples during their annual stay in Newcastle, but there is no certainty that these visits will be repeated.

In the same mould as the Peoples is the **Little Theatre** in Saltwell View, Gateshead (☎478 1499). Again long established, the Little Theatre's work is also adventurous and challenging, and is well patronised by the residents of Gateshead and beyond. Other amateur groups – and there are many – include those in Tynemouth (Priory Arts Group), South Shields (Westovians Theatre Society), Sunderland (Royalty Theatre Group) and Whitley Bay (Playhouse Theatre Group): an astonishing array of activity, considering the problems encountered by professional companies and venues in the area.

YOUNG PEOPLE'S THEATRE

Youth theatre has a high profile on Tyneside. As well as groups in the Tyne and the Peoples, Live Theatre has its own group which it runs in conjunction with the Tyne Theatre Company. An Asian youth group is also based at Live. East of Newcastle, North Tyneside has a strong tradition of youth theatre, based both at the Wallsend Young People's Theatre, and at one of the country's only centres funded solely for young people, Backworth Drama Centre (☎268 4289). Flourishing youth arts groups meet weekly in Gateshead and Sunderland, and youth theatres remain both a stepping-stone to the acting profession, and an exciting means of self expression and simply having fun.

Lastly, the visitor may well be tempted into the beautiful countryside around the population centres. The arts are alive in many tourist centres though Durham City sadly has very little performing arts activity, other than pub bands. The Cathedral occasionally hosts events, notably by the Darlington-based **Durham Theatre Co.** Hexham, the Northumberland market town, has an outstanding Arts Centre, the Queens Hall, a rather upmarket venue. Finally, Alnwick, renowned for its castle, has a theatre, the Playhouse. It mainly stages amateur events but is the base for a professional company, **Northumberland Theatre Co,** whose work is well worth catching.

So, Tyne and Wear – an area not nationally known for its cultural output – contains a wide choice of entertaining venues. The common theme of most theatres described is eclectic programming policies and much behind-the-scenes political intrigue. It was ever thus in the North East.

The prices, admission times and other information given in this guide were correct at the time of going to press, but may be changed by the establishments concerned during the life of the book. While the publishers have made every effort to ensure that the information in this book is accurate, they do not accept any responsibility for mistakes made during its its compilation or for changes made since the information was compiled. They will be very pleased to hear from anyone with information about changes, inaccuracies or omissions: please send details in writing to: *Tyneside: Where's the Buzz*, Bloodaxe Books (Projects) Ltd, P.O. Box 1SN, Newcastle upon Tyne NE99 1SN.

The views expressed in this book on various subjects include those of a number of different contributors. They are not necessarily shared by the editor or by the publishers.

CINEMA

Geordie goes to Hollywood

There are over two dozen cinema screens on Tyneside, enough for even a dedicated film buff to see something different every night of the week, from the newest general releases to esoteric, foreign and classic movies, from *Scandal* and *The Jungle Book* to *Betty Blue* and *Rebel Without a Cause*.

The **Odeon** on Pilgrim Street shows the usual range of mainstream feature films. It is a large four-screen complex, with a shop in the foyer selling posters, cards, videos, sweets and drinks. There are also special Pullman seats if you are prepared to spend a little more for extra comfort. Prices: £2.60 for U, PG and 15 certificate, £2.80 for 18 certificate, and £3.30 for Pullman seats. Reductions are £1.90 for students with an NUS card, £1.75 for senior citizens, children and the unemployed.

● Tyneside Cinema's main auditorium.

Behind the rather scruffy exterior of the **Tyneside Cinema** on Pilgrim Street lies an impressive example of 30s Art Deco architecture. The Tyneside, built in 1937, was originally the News Theatre, showing newsreels and cartoons. In 1986 the interior of the cinema was faithfully restored in the style of the heyday of Hollywood, complete with mosaic floors and elaborate marble-effect ceilings.

This independent arts cinema now offers an interesting and lively alternative to the other general release cinemas. The Tyneside has two screens showing films from all over the world – the widest selection outside London – and hosts an annual film festival in the autumn. The cinema also has its own coffee rooms and bookshop. Sadly, the usherettes no longer wear Tyrolean costumes, but there is still a beautiful red curtain which still goes up and down.

Ticket prices: £2.40 full price, £1.40 for OAPs, disabled and unemployed. Children's screenings £1 (£1.90 for adults), late night films £2.95. All seats are cheaper on Mondays. Consult the Tyneside's own monthly programme for more details.

The two-screen **Cannon** at the bottom of Westgate Road offers the usual selection of feature films at £1.30 for the first three performances and £2.50 for the last. The **Jesmond Cinema** outside West Jesmond metro station is a more traditional picture house built in 1922. The seats are comfortable and reasonably priced at £2 (£1 for children and OAPs). Films showing are general release films on a second run, to give you a chance to see those you missed the first time round, and Disney classics during the school holidays.

For a real flavour of 'Saturday night at the movies', you have a choice of two multi-screen cinema complexes, the new **Multiplex Warner Brothers** cinema at Manors and the **AMC** ten-screen complex at the MetroCentre. The MetroCentre gives you a taste of movie-going American-style. Once you've chosen your film and your hot dogs, sweets and ice cream, and found your screen – which is rather like finding an airport terminal – you'll be grateful for the comfort of your seat. There's a special holder in the arm for your drink, but you'll have to keep your MetroCentre-sized bucket of popcorn on your knee. But be warned: films start bang on time. Before 6pm seats cost £1.95, or £1.75 for kids, and after 6pm the price is £2.95 for everyone.

POETRY

Where's the buzz in poetry? In Britain the answer must be Tyneside: the most important centre for poetry outside London for the past 25 years.

MORDEN TOWER

In 1964 Newcastle poet Tom Pickard set up the Morden Tower poetry readings in a turret room on the old City Wall. He tracked down the great Northumbrian poet Basil Bunting, then living in obscurity in Wylam, and the enthusiastic young Morden Tower audiences encouraged Bunting to start writing again. He composed his epic work *Briggflatts* to show Pickard how to write a long poem, and *Briggflatts* was given its first public reading in 1965, at Morden Tower.

At the height of the poetry explosion of the sixties, visiting American writers like Ginsberg, Ferlinghetti, Creeley and Burroughs would come to Newcastle before London or Liverpool, and Morden Tower still attracts some of the top names in poetry from throughout the world, as well as providing a platform for exciting new talents. The Tower itself isn't very big (it can't comfortably hold more than 100), but its reputation is international.

It's not an easy place to find the first time you go: behind Gallowgate Bus Station, down the dark alley called Back Stowell Street between the City Wall and Rosie's pub in St Andrews Street. The facilities are limited to the chairs, the poet's table and a stove in the winter. The Gents is the alley wall outside; the nearest Ladies is in the pub. Audiences gather before and after readings in the Newcastle Arms in St Andrews Street.

Readings start at 8pm. The three fortnightly seasons run from January to Easter, April to July, and October to Christmas. Ask to be put on the mailing list. For details of the latest programme, write to the organiser, Tony Baynes, at Morden Tower, c/o Dept of English, Dept of Humanities & Science, Newcastle College, Maple Terrace, Newcastle NE4 7SA (☎273 8866 x 2380).

BLOODAXE BOOKS

Britain's premier poetry publisher, Bloodaxe Books, is based in Newcastle, and organises readings and book launches at various venues in the city. Bloodaxe published Russian poet Irina Ratushinskaya's *No, I'm Not Afraid*, the book which spearheaded the international cam-

ARTS 135

paign for her release from a Soviet labour camp. When Irina came to Britain, she gave her first public reading in Newcastle – for Bloodaxe at the Newcastle Playhouse.

Leading British poet Tony Harrison lives in Newcastle, and when Bloodaxe published his controversial poem *v.* – which made front page headlines in the *Daily Mail* and the *Star* – the book was launched at the University's Hatton Gallery. Bloodaxe's legendary 10th birthday marathon reading by 30 poets was held at the Royal Station Hotel.

Each autumn Bloodaxe organises the *Evening Chronicle* Poetry Competition, the only one of its kind in the country, with over £1500 worth of prizes. The winners' reading at the Literary and Philosophical Society in Westgate Road is a major event in Newcastle's literary calendar.

Following the success of *Bossy Parrot*, Bloodaxe's book of the best poems by North-East youngsters submitted to the competition, two young poets "discovered" by the Chronicle have set up the Bloodaxe Young Persons' Poetry Club. Iain Pigg and Elaine Cusack run the Saturday afternoon poetry workshops in Jesmond Library, often with visiting writers. For further details, write to Iain and Elaine c/o Bloodaxe Books.

If you want to be kept informed about Bloodaxe's books and events, ask to be put on the mailing list. Write to Bloodaxe Books, P.O. Box 1SN, Newcastle NE99 1SN (☎232 5988).

TYNESIDE'S POETRY MAGAZINES & PRESSES

Tyneside is buzzing with poetry activity: reading, writing and publishing. Many leading poets live and work in the region, including Tony Harrison, Tom Pickard, Anne Stevenson, Jon Silkin, Alistair Elliot, Gillian Allnutt and Carol Rumens. Tyneside's many literary magazines and presses organise poetry readings. Most have got funny names, but don't let this put you off writing to them for details of their publications, competitions, readings, talks and workshops:

Stand: *179 Wingrove Road, Fenham, Newcastle NE4 9DA* (☎273 3280) 'Stand' as in making a stand, a platform for new writing. Founded in 1952, *Stand* is a prestigious international quarterly magazine of poetry and short stories edited by poet Jon Silkin and Virago fiction writer Lorna Tracy, also publishing poetry collections under its **Northern House** imprint.

The Echo Room: *45 Bewick Court, Princess Sq, Newcastle NE1 8EG* (☎261 5791). One of the country's liveliest magazines of new poetry. Edited by Irish poet Brendan Cleary, its publishing line is radical, disrespectful and urgent. **Echo Room Press** publishes zappy collections by exciting new poets.

Iron: *5 Marden Tce, Cullercoats NE30 4PD* (☎253 1901). Edited by local journalist Peter Mortimer, *Iron* provides a lively forum for new writers and artists, and does much to publicise new writing from the North East. **Iron Press** publishes poetry, fiction and drama books.

Writing Women: *7 Cavendish Place, Newcastle NE2 2NE.* (☎281 6986). Exactly what it says, and the only women's literary magazine in Britain. Edited by Linda Anderson, Cynthia Fuller and Jo Alberti.

Pig Press: *7 Cross View Terrace, Neville's Cross, Durham DH1 4JY* (☎384 6914). Nothing to do with pigs but an international "modernist" press set up by poet Ric Caddel to publish British and American avant-garde literature.

Galloping Dog Press: *45 Salisbury*

Gardens, Newcastle NE2 1HP (☎281 7838). Small press pioneer Peter Hodgkiss keeps them doggies rolling, and the dogs in question are nosing ahead of the avant-garde.
Jonathon: *16 Poplar Grove, Flint Hill, Stanley DH9 9BE*. Tyneside's newest, youngest press edited by the eager Iain Pigg. **Jonathon Press** is its pamphlet imprint.
Poetry Durham: *c/o Department of English, Elvet Riverside, New Elvet, Durham DH1 3JT* (☎386 4466). Not Durham poetry but a national magazine edited from Durham by poets Gareth Reeves and Michael O'Neill.
Panurge: *22 Belle Grove West, Newcastle NE2 4LT* (☎232 7669). Not a laxative but a quality literary magazine, one of the few devoted entirely to new fiction, edited by short story writer David Almond.

And you thought Bloodaxe was a funny name! (as in Viking King Eric Bloodaxe, last ruler of the independent North).

OTHER POETRY VENUES

Morden Tower is the main place for readings. Poetry events are also held at several other venues, often in conjunction with the presses and magazines listed above:
First Wave: A new fringe-type festival organised by Newcastle City Council in July 'promoting arts, youth and enterprise', including a mini literature festival run by young people for young people (director Geoff Brown, ☎261 0691).
Caedmon Hall: *Gateshead Central Library, Prince Consort Rd, Gateshead NE8 4JB* (Alison Lister, ☎477 3478). Varied programme running throughout the year including many community-based events, sometimes part of a week-long festival.
Side Cinema: *9 Side, Newcastle NE1 3JE* (Kitty Fitzgerald, ☎232 2208). Mainly women writers, political writers and northerners.
Colpitts Poetry: *Bridge Hotel, North Rd, Durham*. Durham is only 20 minutes from Newcastle by train, and Colpitts readings often feature some of the country's best poets. Their original home was the Colpitts pub; the new venue, the Bridge Hotel, is just below the viaduct by Durham railway station. Information from Michael Ayton, 19 Mitchell St, Durham (☎384 0793).
Projects UK: *1 Black Swan Court, Newcastle Arts Centre, Westgate Rd, Newcastle NE1 1SG* (☎232 2410). Experimental writers and performance poets, often with music.
Live Theatre: *Broad Chare, Quayside, Newcastle NE1 3DF* (Paul Rubinstein, ☎261 2694). Lunchtime and late night performance poetry.
Broken Doll: *85 Blenheim St, Newcastle NE1 4BW* (☎232 1047). Wild, wacky and outrageous poetry performers included in alternative pub cabaret. Not to be missed except when they're so wild they're downright disgusting.
Tyneside Poets: c/o Alan Brown (☎286 2129). Local writers.

Much of the poetry activity on Tyneside is supported and publicised by Northern Arts. For further information contact Jenny Attala, Literature Officer, Northern Arts, 9-10 Osborne Tce, Newcastle NE2 1NZ (☎281 6634). Northern Arts have detailed information about local writers' groups and writers' workshop schemes run in local libraries and community centres. For the latest information on performance poetry nights in pubs and other venues, see the listings magazines *Index* and *Paint It Red*.

CLASSICAL MUSIC

The music scene on Tyneside is dominated by the **Northern Sinfonia**, a chamber orchestra of 35 to 40 players, founded 30 years ago by Michael Hall. Small enough to appear in the region's more modest venues, it is large enough to cope with much of the 19th century repertoire from Beethoven to Schubert onwards, and with a good deal of 20th century music. Commissions from young composers, particularly those with strong North-East connections, are a feature of their programmes.

Over the years the Sinfonia has had a succession of distinguished artistic directors – among them Rudolf Schwartz, Tamas Vasary and Ivan Fischer – all of whom have made their mark on the character and development of the orchestra. During his seven years as director, Richard Hickox has taken the Sinfonia to many of the country's leading festivals and added considerably to its list of gramophone recordings, which range from Elgar and Britten under Sir Neville Marriner to a complete Beethoven symphony cycle under Hickox himself. From May 1990 the Sinfonia's Artistic Director is to be the celebrated cellist Heinrich Schiff, whose impact as a conductor in the orchestra's 1988/89 season was immediate.

Many renowned soloists have been brought to Tyneside by the Sinfonia – among them Tortelier, Menuhin and Perahia – and the orchestra is well-known internationally, having toured extensively throughout Europe and in North and South America.

There are at least a dozen Sinfonia concerts each season in the City Hall, and the orchestra regularly visits other main centres in the North such as Darlington, Stockton, Middlesbrough, Carlisle and Kendal, with a wide range of programmes, many of them planned by associate conductor and principal flautist, David Haslam. He has also played a prominent part in fostering the enjoyment of music in young people, and each season a number of children's concerts are given at the Newcastle Playhouse.

In recent years the Sinfonia have become specialists, under the direction of percussionist Alan Fearon, in music for silent films, and have played for Abel Gance's epic *Napoleon* (music by Beethoven/Carl Davis), for *The Italian Straw Hat* and for Eisenstein's *October*. Alan Fearon also trains the Sinfonia Chorus who make frequent appearances in concerts and broadcasts with the orchestra. Chamber music, too, forms part of the Sinfonia's

● Opera at the Theatre Royal: Jorge Pita and Nancy Gustafson in Scottish Opera's production of *La Traviata*.

commitment to the region, with both wind and string ensembles playing regularly for music clubs in the region and throughout the country.

Visiting orchestras such as the Hallé and Scottish National, and continental orchestras such as the Czech and Warsaw Philharmonic, provide heavier symphonic fare at the City Hall, in a series centred on the 19th century. The concerts, organised by **Eric Caller**, feature orchestral masterpieces by composers such as Beethoven, Mahler, Bruckner and Elgar.

The **Newcastle Chamber Music Society** has a long and distinguished history. Founded in 1880, it has hosted many of the world's leading string quartets, and continues to promote around six concerts a year by leading ensembles such as the Bartok Quartet and the Endellion Quartet, the Nash Ensemble and the Stuttgart Piano Trio. After many years in the august surroundings of the old Assembly Rooms – now, sadly, no longer available – the Society moved to Newcastle University's King's Hall, but currently holds its concerts in the Playhouse, with sponsorship from English Estates.

The **Newcastle University Music Department** has survived two recent threats to its existence from university cutbacks and continues to make a valuable contribution to the cultural life of the region, with a series of lunchtime concerts on Tuesdays (given primarily by students) and Thursdays (with visiting artists) during term time. In addition the Department mounts two orchestral concerts a year, and there are public concerts by the Choir and by the Madrigal Choir. All these events, like the public lectures – a highlight of the University calendar since the late Denis Matthews' term of office as Professor of Music – attract enthusiastic support from both town and gown. The **Bach Choir** and orchestra may be heard several times in the season in the choral masterpieces of Bach, Handel, Mozart and Tippett, etc, under the direction of Dr Eric Cross, usually in King's Hall but also occasionally in the Cathedral.

Dr Cross also directs the smaller **Cappella Novocastriensis** in classical and pre-classical music. The **Camerata Singers** and the **Tyneside Chamber Orchestra**, under the direction of Percy Lovell – a former lecturer at Newcastle – give occasional concerts in the city and also visit smaller venues in outlying areas. The **New Tyneside Orchestra**, under Stephen Pettitt, is a large amateur organisation which usually performs in King's Hall, often with a visiting soloist. An annual summer event at the City Hall is the performance given by the **Northern Junior Philharmonic Orchestra** after a week's intensive training and coaching under expert professional guidance. A high point of the 1988 season was a magnificent performance of Messiaen's *Turangalila* symphony.

Other less central venues include the **Peoples Theatre** in Heaton: their flourishing music society has been active for over 40 years and provides six concerts during the season, with the accent (though not exclusively so) on British talent – visitors in past seasons have included artists such as Julian Bream, John Lill and the Fitzwilliam String Quartet. At the **Literary and Philosophical Society** on Lower Westgate Road there is a series of monthly Monday lunchtime recitals, organised since 1979 by Noel Broome, for which performers give their services free. Programmes range from piano recitals to a wide variety of vocal and instrumental music (a new grand piano was bought, specifically for the series, in 1988). At Rye Hill, off Westgate Road, the School of Music attached to the **Newcastle College** has a fine, small, purpose-built concert hall where performances are usually open to the public.

There is a strong choral tradition in the North East; the **Festival**

Chorus, under Len Young, is a large body of singers occasionally assembled for performances of major choral works in the City Hall, often with a visiting orchestra. (Len Young is Newcastle Education's director of music and he is active in promoting both vocal and instrumental concerts by young people.) A number of fine churches in the region, among them St James and St Basil's in Fenham, St George's in Jesmond, St Thomas's in the Haymarket and, of course, the Cathedral Church of St Nicholas – home of the celebrated 19th century musician, Charles Avison – provide ideal settings for a number of choral concerts, as well as providing opportunities for visiting organists in various recitals during the year.

Grand opera may be heard, usually at the Theatre Royal, at least three times a year, with visits from **Scottish Opera** and items from their main repertory, and productions of established masterpieces by Verdi, Puccini, Weber, etc, by **Northern Opera**; the latter are impressively mounted and sung, often by local talent and accompanied by a professional orchestra. Scottish Opera's superb week-long programmes are always sold out months in advance, leaving opera lovers to ask why seasons by Scottish Opera or other nationally renowned opera companies can't be staged more frequently in a theatre which loses money on poorly supported shows at other times of the year. The Theatre Royal also hosts highly popular occasional visits from leading ballet companies such as **Sadlers Wells Royal Ballet** and the **London Festival Ballet**.

Twenty miles west of Newcastle the market town of Hexham supports the annual summer **Hexham Music Festival** centred on the ancient abbey, with its fine 1974 Phelps organ. This is a long-established communal festival with much use of local talent (recent events have included, for example, performances of Britten's *Noyes Fludde*) topped up by distinguished visiting artists; in its early years the festival was visited by artists of the calibre of Britten, Pears and Brannigan. The highlight of the festival is usually a major choral and orchestral work in the Abbey, with the Northern Sinfonia and top-flight soloists; other orchestral concerts and recitals are held there during the festival, and in smaller venues such as the Queen's Hall Arts Centre, the Wentworth Leisure Centre and the High School.

LIVE MUSIC

Tyneside is one of the liveliest places in the country for rock, blues, jazz and folk music. It's not just known as the home of the Animals, Lindisfarne, Hank Marvin, Sting and Bryan Ferry – and of TV's much lamented *Tube* – but is also seen as the breeding ground for many of today's exciting new bands, from Prefab Sprout, Hurrah and the Kane Gang to And All Because the Lady Loves, Quinn the Eskimo, the Anthill Runners, and Martin Stephenson and the Daintees. Many of the new bands have records from thriving local labels like Kitchenware, Desert Sounds, Neat, Woosh, and Paint It Red.

The folk revival started at venues like Newcastle's Bridge Folk Club, and over the years the region has produced some of the country's best known traditional and contemporary folk musicians: Lindisfarne and Jack the Lad, the High Level Ranters and Alistair Anderson, Vin Garbutt, the Teesside Fettlers, Prelude and Kathryn Tickell.

The North East is also a hot spot for jazz and blues, with the international Newcastle Jazz Festival running for a week every May and Gateshead's Jazz Festival in October, and popular outfits like the River City Jazzmen, the Tyne Valley Stompers, the West Jesmond Rhythm Kings, Little Mo and Ray Stubbs' R&B Allstars playing around the region throughout the year. Also in May, the North Shields Fishquay Festival has all-day programmes of live music throughout the bank holiday weekend.

There are also *really big* concerts staged from time to time at St James's Park, when you can catch the music not just in the ground but all over Tyneside! The Rolling Stones, Bruce Springsteen and Bob Dylan have all played to capacity crowds at St James's Park.

Fans travel all over the North East to catch their favourite bands, and to hear music by new and up-and-coming groups. The regular venues include pubs, clubs and arts centres: these are listed below, with contact names for information about what's on at each venue. For the very latest on who the buzz bands are and where they're playing, pick up a copy of *Paint It Red* at Volume Records, or take out a subscription (£5 a year from CNA, 13 North Tce, Claremont Rd, Newcastle NE2 4AD. ☎261 1902). There's now only one other listings magazine, the Northern Arts sponsored *Index*, whose coverage is more general. For more info on **Riverside**, the region's top rock venue, see the Clubs section of this guide.

ROCK VENUES

Balancing Eel: Ocean Rd, South Shields. *Tony White,* ☎ 456 1710.
Barley Mow: Sandgate, Newcastle. *Fred Plater, Ian Thompson,* ☎232 3114.
The Barn: Leazes Park Rd, Newcastle. *Rose,* ☎261 6373.
Blue Monkey: Bedford St, Sunderland. *Rico,* ☎510 9134.
The Borough: Vine Place, Sunderland. *Bob,* ☎567 7909.
Brewery Arts Centre: Highgate, Kendal, Cumbria. *Jonny Smith, Sheila Mason,* ☎0539-25133.
Bridge Hotel: Castle Sq (next to High Level Bridge), Newcastle. ☎232 7780.
Broken Doll: Blenheim St, Newcastle. *Martin,* ☎232 1047.
Buddle Arts Centre: Station Rd, Wallsend. *Martin Dower,* ☎262 4276.
Caedmon Hall: Prince Consort Rd, Gateshead. *June O'Malley,* ☎477 3478.
Community Arts Centre: c/o Crossgate Club, behind North Rd, Durham. *Mark Butcher,* ☎386 8176/386 9576.
Cooperage: The Close, Quayside, Newcastle. ☎232 8286.
Corner House: Heaton Rd, Newcastle. ☎265 9602.
Darlington Arts Centre: Vane Tce, Darlington. *Ian Hague,* ☎0325-483168.
Dovecot Arts Centre: Dovecot St, Stockton. *William Jones,* ☎0642-611625.
Dunelm House: New Elvet, Durham. *Bruno Jordan,* ☎374 3320.
Eustace Percy Hall: Castle Leazes (Newcastle University), Spital Tongues, Newcastle. *Dave Allsop,* ☎232 8511 x 8421.
Fiddlers Three: Albion St, Felling. ☎469 2219.
Forth: Pink Lane, Newcastle. *Lee Conlan,* ☎261 1902/222 1414.
Fowlers Yard Youth Project: Back Silver St, Durham. *Lillian Sherington,* ☎386 9576.
Freeman Hall: Castle Leazes (Newcastle University), Spital Tongues, Newcastle. *Martin Dunn,* ☎232 8511 x 8404/8327.
Free Trade Inn: St Lawrence Rd, below Byker. ☎265 5764.
Front Page: Fisher St, Carlisle. ☎0228-34168.
Gatsbys: Olive St, Sunderland. *Mr Fairley, Mrs Lucy Young,* ☎510 9634.
Havelock Hall: Castle Leazes (Newcastle University), Spital Tongues, Newcastle. *Mark Daley, Chris Wood,* ☎232 8511 x 8300.
Inn on the Park: Barrack Rd, Newcastle. ☎261 0777.
Jewish Mother: Leazes Arcade, Newcastle. *Mike Gosney,* ☎261 4060.
Kazbah: George St (off Roker Ave), Monkwearmouth, Sunderland. *Dave Thompson,* ☎510 8890
Kirklevington Country Club: Thirsk Rd, Yarm, Cleveland. *Mr Bell,* ☎0642-780345.
Luckies Bar: St Mary's Place, Newcastle. ☎232 3893.
Mayfair: Low Friar St, Newcastle. *Brian Hopson, Derek Hewes,* ☎232 3109. *See entry in Clubs section.*
Middlesbrough Town Hall: Albert Rd, Middlesbrough. *Mike Body, Jean Hewitt.* ☎0642-221866.
Morpeth Court House: Castle Bank, Morpeth. *Mr Patterson or Carol,* ☎0670-511270.
New Crown Hotel: Mowbray Rd, South Shields. *Mrs Biggs,* ☎455 2213.
Newcastle Arts Centre: Lower Westgate Rd, Newcastle. *Mike Tilley, Richard Jardine,* ☎261 5618.
Newcastle City Hall: Northumberland Rd, Newcastle. ☎261 2606.
Newcastle Playhouse: Barras Bridge, Newcastle. *Mr Taylor,*

☎261 0703.
Puzzles: Grand Hotel, Grand Parade, Tynemouth. *Mike Goodman,* ☎257 2106.
Queens Hall Arts Centre: Beaumont St, Hexham. *Mylee Hall, Graham McKinnon,* ☎0434 607272.
Red House: Sandhill, Quayside, Newcastle. *Peter Scott, Barry Hunt,* ☎261 0921.
Riverside: Melbourne St, Newcastle. *Babs Johnson,* ☎261 4386. See entry in *Clubs* section.
Ship in the Hole: Gainors Tce, Wallsend. ☎262 3854.
Sinatras: Holmside, Sunderland. *Peter,* ☎565 7604.
Surfers Bar: Seafront, Tynemouth. *Peter,* ☎257 6053/276 6758.
Vedcar Bowl: Majuba Rd, Redcar. *Christina Wicks,* ☎231 212.
Walkers Club Café: Low Friar St, Newcastle. *Keith Gordon,* ☎232 3303. See entry in *Clubs* section.
Washington Arts Centre: Biddick Lane, Fatfield, Washington. *Adam Sutherland,* ☎416 6440.
Waterfront: Castlegate Quay, Riverside, Stockton. *Peter Crossen,* ☎0642-674309.
White Swan: Morpeth. ☎0670-513532.
Wolsington House: Burdon Main Row (next to Smith's ship repair yard), North Shields. ☎257 8487.
The Works: Nelson St, Consett. ☎0207-590564.
Zefferelli's: Ambleside, Cumbria. *Derek Hook,* ☎0539-433845.
Zoots: Waterloo St, Newcastle. *Sonya,* ☎261 4507. See entry in *Clubs* section.

JAZZ VENUES

MONDAY
Black House: Windy Nook. *Black House Rag Time Orchestra.*
Broken Doll: Blenheim St, Newcastle. *Stangers Blunt End:* traditional jazz and Chicago blues.

TUESDAY
Bridge Hotel: Castle Sq (next to High Level Bridge), Newcastle. *Jumpin' & Hot Club:* various bands. (8pm)
Corner House: Heaton Rd, Newcastle.
Lonsdale: opposite West Jesmond metro, Newcastle. *River City Jazzmen.* (8pm)
Porthole: New Quay, North Shields. *Porthole Jazzmen.*
Ravensdene Lodge: Lobley Hill, Gateshead. *Tyne Valley Stompers.* (8.30pm, admission £1)
Wolsington House: Burdon Main Row (next to Smith's ship repair yard), North Shields. *Mississippi Dreamboats.*

WEDNESDAY
Corner House: Heaton Rd, Newcastle. *Mike Waller Trio.*
Fiddlers Three: Albion St, Windy Nook. *Vintage Jazzmen.*
Old Mill Country Club: Tursdale. *Dick Straughan Sextet featuring Jude Murphy.*

THURSDAY
Black Bull: Bridge St, Blaydon. *Bill Smith, Roly Veitch.* (8.30pm)
Corner House: Heaton Rd, Newcastle.
High Point Hotel: Promenade, Whitley Bay. *West Jesmond Rhythm Kings.* (8pm, admission free)
Rose, Shamrock & Thistle: Streetgate, Sunniside. *Tyne Valley Stompers.*

FRIDAY
Crown & Thistle: North Rd, Catchgate, Stanley. Various jazz bands. (8.30–11pm, admission £1)

SATURDAY
Broadway Ballroom: Pelaw. *Dick*

Straughan Band, and special guests. (Occasional Saturdays only)

SUNDAY
Broken Doll: Blenheim St, Newcastle. Traditional jazz & Chicago blues: *Stangers Blunt End*. (Afternoon & 8pm)
Corner House: Heaton Rd, Newcastle.
New Crown Hotel: Mowbray Rd, South Shields. *South Tyne Jazz Club:* various bands. (8.30pm)
Rose, Shamrock & Thistle: Streetgate, Sunniside. *Tyne Valley Stompers*.

BLUES VENUES

MONDAY
Corner House: Heaton Rd, Newcastle. *Ray Stubbs R&B Allstars*.

TUESDAY
Free Trade Inn: St Lawrence Rd, below Byker. Various acts.
Potters Wheel: Front St, Sunniside. R&B bands.

WEDNESDAY
Rose & Crown: South Shields. Various acts.

THURSDAY
Castletown Inn: Sunderland. Various acts.
Crossgate Club: Durham. R&B bands.
Harveys: Stockton. *Ray Stubbs R&B Allstars*.
Kazbah: George St (off Roker Ave), Monkwearmouth, Sunderland. R&B bands.

FRIDAY
Mowbray Park Hotel: Borough Rd, Sunderland. R&B bands.
Rose Tree: Durham City. R&B bands.

SUNDAY
Borough Arms: Sunderland. Various acts.
Broken Doll: Blenheim St, Newcastle. Various acts (lunchtime). R&B bands (evening).

FOLK VENUES

MONDAY
Gainford Folk Club: Lord Nelson, Gainford. ☎0325-315679.
Lambton Hounds Folk Club: Lambton Hounds, Pity Me, near Durham. ☎584 7652.
Last Resort: The Victoria, Saltburn. ☎0287-33173.
Lord Nelson: Monkton Village, Jarrow. ☎489 1758.
Old George's Music Box: Old George Inn, Cloth Mkt, Newcastle. ☎232 3956.
Staindrop: Black Swan, Staindrop, Bishop Auckland.
Stockton Folk Club: Sun Inn, Knowles St, Stockton. ☎0642-815233.

TUESDAY
Albert: Albert Rd, Middlesbrough. ☎0287-77453.
Black Lion: Sedgefield. ☎0740-20149.
Chester-le-Street: LMC Cricket Club (off Main St), Chester-le-St. ☎388 6156.
Darlington Folk: The Britannia, Archer St, Darlington. ☎0325-465613.
Hen Knowle Manor: Bishop Auckland. *Singaround, 8.30pm*.
Plough Folk: The Plough, Middle Farm, Cramlington. ☎0670-737633.
Tavern Folk Club: Railway Tavern, Cramlington. ☎0670-715532.

WEDNESDAY
Birtley Folk Club: RAOB CIU Club,

off Main St, Birtley. *Peter Elliott (work),* ☎232 8511 x 2203.
Cumberland Arms: Byker. *Bar session.* ☎265 5151.
East Durham Folk Club: Kings Head, Easington. ☎0429-276761.
Glebe LMC: The Royalty, Chester Rd, Sunderland. ☎567 6876.
Rocking Horse: Station Rd, Hexham. *Singers' Night.* ☎0434-603155.
Victory: New Hartley.
Wackerfield Folk Club: Sun Inn, Wackerfield, Co. Durham. *Last Wednesday in the month.* ☎0338-718813/718205.
Wheatsheaf: Carlisle St, Felling. *Bar session.* ☎436 6633.

THURSDAY
Ashington: Folk Bar, Leisure Centre, Institute Rd, Ashington. *Ken Self,* ☎0670 812604.
Belford House: Belford House Sports Club, Sunderland. ☎0783-84237.
Bridge Folk Club (Folk Song & Ballad): Bridge Hotel, Castle Sq (next to High Level Bridge), Newcastle. ☎284 3693.
Crown: Hedworth, Boldon Colliery. *Free session.* ☎567 3994
Darlington Folk Song Club: Arts Centre, Vane Tce, Darlington. ☎0325-281746.
Durham City: Bridge Hotel (nr station), Durham. ☎386 5754.
Holystone Folk Club: The Holystone Inn, Whitley Rd, Holystoné, nr Shiremoor. ☎266 3684.

Queens Arms: Acomb, nr Hexham. *Singaround.*

FRIDAY
Buddlefolk: Buddle Arts Centre, Station Rd, Wallsend. *Alternate Fridays.* ☎262 4276.
Folkstyle: Montalbo Hotel, Barnard Castle. ☎0325-730195.
Red Lion: Trimdon Village. ☎0915-862425.
South Tyne Music Club: Douglas Vaults, South Shields. ☎0916-675994.
White Swan: Greenside, Ryton. *Singaround.* ☎413 4255.

SATURDAY
Davy Lamp Folk Club: Washington Arts Centre, Biddick Farm, Fatfield, Washington. ☎416 6999.

SUNDAY
Adam & Eve: The Ship, Wylam. ☎413 5330.
Bay Folk Club: Bay Hotel, Cullercoats. ☎252 1380.
Collingwood: The Collingwood (near railway station), Thornaby. ☎0642-557098.
Guisborough: Rugby Club, Belmangate, Guisborough. ☎0287-24692.
Hartlepool: Nursery Inn, Hart Lane, Hartlepool. ☎0429-262808.
Marsden: Marsden .Inn, South Shields. ☎0783-671617.
Seaham: Golden Lion Hotel, Railway St, Seaham Harbour.
South Hetton: Station Hotel, South Hetton. ☎526 2397

COUNTRY & WESTERN
MONDAY: **Cleadon & District WMC:** South Shields; **South Shields Unionist Club:** South Shields.
TUESDAY: **Geordie Ridley:** Blaydon; **Marine Hotel,** South Shields; **Old Cross Inn,** Ryton.
THURSDAY: **Ship,** Whitley Bay.
FRIDAY: **Brigham & Cowans,** South Shields; **Ashington Northern WMC,** Ashington; **Companions Club,** Wallsend.
SATURDAY: **Jarrow Labour Club,** Park Road; **Ovington Social Club,** Prudhoe.
SUNDAY: **Broadway,** Pelaw; **Six Mile Bridge,** Seaton Burn; **Iona,** Hebburn.

SPORT

There is so much sport on Tyneside that we can only scratch the surface in this guide. But here, at least, are some starting points...

ANGLING

Tweedswood Enterprises: *Kirkwhelpington, Northumberland.* ☎0830-40341
Trout fishing on Great Sweethope, Little Sweethope or Linnheads. Season: 22 March–31 October. Mornings £6 per rod, double session £11 per rod. Three fish limit.

Westwater Angling: *Whittle Dene Reservoirs, Stamfordham.* ☎0434681-405
This angling club is open from 8am until dusk. Tickets are available on a self-service basis from the booking-in hut next to the reservoir superintendent's house. Day tickets: £9 per day (inc. VAT).

BOATS

Browns Boathouse: *The Boathouse, Durham. Rebecca Claricoates,* ☎386 9525.
Boating on the River Wear below Durham Cathedral. Rowing boats £1.20/hr per person. Trips all year round on the *Prince Bishop*, a large boat which holds 150 people. No need to book.

Gatsbys Bar on the Bridlington Queen. *Simon & David Gillespie,* ☎285 7229 or 0860-275422
This pleasure boat sails from Newcastle Quayside to the mouth of the Tyne, or to the Stella power station. It leaves on Friday and Saturday nights at 7pm on a three-hour round trip, with a bar on board, and carries up to 120 people.

MFV New Venture: *Owner Gordon Ballard,* ☎258 4306
Fishing trips, birdwatching trips, sightseeing, diving, for up to 12 people, from a 40 foot boat. £8 for inshore fishing, 8.30am–5pm, pick up from North Shields Ice Factory or Mill Dam on south side. £12 for wreck fishing (no bait) from same pick-up points. 10–12 miles out to sea for bigger fish. £60 for trips (whole boat, not per person). The owner is the regional secretary of the National Federation of Chartered Skippers.

The Shieldsman: *summer evening trips,* ☎261 0431 x 229, *private hire, Alan Parks,* ☎454 8183
This Tyne ferry boat is available for ticket sightseeing trips or for private parties. To hire privately, the cost is £474 from Newcastle Quayside to South Shields, Tynemouth and back; or £330 from South Shields to Tynemouth, Newcastle Quayside and back. It holds up to 200 people, so the cost can be cheap if you have enough people. For sightseeing trips, tickets cost £7, which includes a disco, bar and supper. It operates once a week on summer evenings for three months. There are also sightseeing trips on Sunday afternoons in the school holidays: from South Shields to North Shields, Newcastle Quayside and back, with tea and coffee but no bar; price £2 adults, £1 children/OAPs, £6 family ticket.

BOWLING

GX Superbowl: *Garden Wk, Metro-Centre, Gateshead.* ☎460 0444
28-lane ten-pin bowling alley open seven days a week: Mon–Sat, 10am–12pm; Sun, 12am–12pm. Costs: weekdays, adults £1.65, children, £1, nights, £1.35; weekends, adults & children, £1.75; plus 50p shoe hire. Licensed bar area, Queen Victoria pub, pool room, video and amusement arcade are all on the same site.

Newcastle Bowl: *Westgate Rd, Fenham, Newcastle.* ☎273 0236
Open seven days a week, 10am–12pm. 16 lanes. Prices: daytime, adults £1.30 (shoes 55p), juniors £1.10 (shoes 28p); after 6pm, £1.50 for everyone (55p shoes). It runs tournaments, has adult leagues and a junior programme; invites large companies (e.g. Gas Board) to play on Tuesday and Wednesday evenings free of charge; and puts on children's birthday parties.

BOWLS

Gateshead Indoor Bowling Centre: *Gladstone Tce, Gateshead.* ☎477 3269
Eight greens on artificial turf. Membership: £8 per season (Sept–May); veterans £4 per season; spectators 35p. Open 10.30am–10.30pm. Playing fee: before 6.30pm, members 50p & non-members 85p for two hours; after 6.30pm, members 95p & non-members £1.25. Special matches (league): members £1.50, non-members £2. Locker fees: £1.25 per person. Visitors welcome any time. Bar and café facilities.

South Tyneside Indoor Bowls & Social Club: *Jack Clark Recreation Ground, Horsley Hill Rd, South Shields.* ☎454 2023
Eight rink indoor green with two outdoor greens. Admission: members 60p for two hours before 6pm, £1 later. Non-members: add 50p. Shoe and bowl hire 25p each. Membership: £25 p.a; social member, £4.50; veteran, £16. Open: Mond–Wed, 10.30am–10.30pm; Fri–Sun, 10am–10.30pm.

CLIMBING

Most Northumberland crags are on private land (and permission to climb there has to be sought from the owners). The major exceptions are Simonside, Crag Lough and Peel Crag. Most of the crags are in the Cheviots or in the Alnwick and Rothbury area. They are graded according to difficulty from Moderate, through Difficult and various grades of Severe, to Extreme. No climber should set off without a copy of the Northumbrian Mountaineering Club's *Northumberland Climbing Guide* (1989 fifth edition, £8.95), available from climbing shops such as the LD Mountain Centre, Dean St, Newcastle (☎232 3561). For practice, there are indoor climbing walls at the Concordia Sports Centre (Cramlington), Crowtree Leisure Centre (Sunderland), Dolphin Leisure Centre (Darlington) and Thorns Farm, Whickham (Gateshead).

Northumbrian Mountaineering Club: *Secretary Peter Maguire, 6 Highfield Place, Brunswick Green, Wideopen, Newcastle.* ☎236 4577.
Wanneys Climbing Club: *c/o Mike Winter, Flat 4, Akenside Tce, Jesmond, Newcastle.*

CRICKET

McEwans Indoor Cricket Centre: *Rainton Bridge Industrial Estate, Mercantile Rd, Houghton-le-Spring.* ☎584 8630
Open: 10am–10pm. Cricket during the winter: after 5pm, £9.50/hr, or £16 with coach; before 5pm, £7/hr, or £10 with coach.

Northumberland CCC: *Osborne Ave, Jesmond, Newcastle.* ☎281 0775
Although a members' club, anyone can go to watch matches free of charge, except for county matches, for which tickets cost £1 for adults (50p concessions). The highlight of the season is the Callers exhibition fixture in August of two one-day matches played by teams drawn from the England side and current international Test players. Northumberland is a Minor County team, but does play some matches against Championship counties in the preliminary rounds of some of the knockout competitions, and the Minor Counties also form a team for some competitions and play some matches at Jesmond. Neighbouring Durham CCC (☎386 9959) is a Minor County now vying for a place in the County Championship.

DIVING

There are over 550 dive sites and 300 wrecks off the North-East coast. The shipwrecks include some famous vessels from the 19th century as well as First and Second World War ships in various states of decay. In 1838 Grace Darling and her father carried out their daring rescue mission to the *Forfarshire*, the remains of which are off the Farne Islands. The wreck of the paddle-steamer *Pegasus*, which sank in 1843 with the loss of 54 lives, is on the Goldstone rocks off Holy Island. The passenger steamer *SS Stanley* foundered on the Black Middens in the mouth of the Tyne in 1858, along with a schooner which went to its rescue, and there are several wrecks off Tynemouth and South Shields (with diving there controlled by the Harbour Master). For a full description of all the diving sites in the region, see *The Divers Guide to the North-East Coast* by Peter Collings (Collings & Brodie, £7.95).

Aquanautics: *26 Blackcap Close, Ayton, Washington. Alan Nicholson,* ☎417 7196
Sells and hires diving equipment. Tuition varies from £25 to £250. Full set of equipment costs £25 per day. Sports diving, not deep sea.

Diving Centre: *Westgate Rd, Newcastle,* ☎232 7983; *Garden Walk, MetroCentre, Gateshead,* ☎460 9774
Full equipment hire, including wet suit and air bottle, £45 per day, £60 per weekend, £190 per week, or individual items hired separately. Arranges dives and runs a diving school (inc. introductory courses). Open: 9.30am–5.30pm; Thurs, till 7pm; Wed, closed.

Whitley Bay Diving Centre: *Whitley Rd, Whitley Bay.* ☎253 4235
Full equipment hire, including wet suit and air bottle, £27.50 per day. Runs a six-week course at Killingworth Baths: £85 including all equipment. Open: 9.30am–5.30pm.

FLYING & PARACHUTING

Aero Club Ltd: *Woolsington, Newcastle. Flight office,* ☎286 1321. *Club house,* ☎286 9447
New members must be nominated

SPORT 149

by existing members. The annual subscription is £12 (inc. VAT), plus a £15 initial joining fee. The flying rate per hour is £61.

Northumbria Gliding Club: *Currock Hill, Chopwell.* ☎0207-561286
Open to visitors. Winch launch height 1000ft, lasts 5 minutes and costs £5. Aerotow to 2000ft lasts 20 minutes and costs £15. Open: 9am–5pm weekends only and Wednesday evenings in summer. Membership £55 plus entry fee £35. Membership entitles you to launches at £1.80 and £9 for Aerotow.

Northumbrian Microlights: *Eshott Airfield, nr Felton.* ☎258 0982
Training school for light aircraft flying. Hourly rate depends upon previous experience. Runs a variety of courses.

Reed Aviation: *Market Place, Alnwick.* ☎0665-6025005
Sightseeing flights in a four-seater Cessna light aircraft from Newcastle Airport. 20 minute flight around Tyneside, £12.50 per passenger. 40 minute Northumbria airtour at £25 per passenger takes you north to Alnwick, Bamburgh and the Farnes, returning via Seahouses, Craster, Alnmouth, Warkworth, Amble and Newbiggin. Three passengers needed for a booking. Captain Eric Reed also operates a business charter service to any airfield in the country at £105/hr, and VIP charter tours of northern England.

Skydive Action: *158 Durham Rd, Gateshead.* ☎478 7289
Parachuting takes place at Embleton where you can be trained to do charity parachute jumps. Weekend training, with jumps completed on Saturday afternoon or Sunday morning. The cost is £50 for charity fundraisers; the course is free if you raise £120 in sponsorship. The cost is £80 (including kit hire) if you're not jumping for charity, with training up to free fall standard. The price for qualified jumpers is linked to the height of the drop. BPA standard. Non-members welcome.

Windlord Hang Gliding School: *Home Farm Cottages, Swarland, Northumberland.* ☎067087-774
Registered BHGA school which provides all equipment needed. Early flights are taken on gentle slopes in special training gliders. BHGA compulsory membership: £15. Two-day introductory course: £68. Elementary Pilot Certificate (5 to 6 days): £170. Club Pilot Certificate; £34/day. Discount for groups of more than five. Windlord operates all year round, and runs flying holidays to the Pyrenees.

FOOTBALL

Newcastle United Football Club: *St James's Park, Newcastle.* ☎232 8561
Prices: West Stand, £9, £8, £7, £6.50; East Stand, £9, £7 on wings. Standing: adults £4, juveniles £2. Invalid section: £4. Season tickets: West Stand, £190, £170, £150, £130, £120; East Stand, £160, £140. No season tickets for standing. The ground opens at 1.30pm on Saturdays in the season (August to May). Newcastle Reserves play on alternate Wednesdays: West Stand, £1; rest if stadium is closed.

GOLF

Arcot Hall Golf Club: *Dudley, Cramlington.* ☎236 2794
Six miles north of Newcastle near

the junction of the Tyne Tunnel road and the Great North Road. The course is 18 holes, par 70. Green fees: £12 per day midweek. For booking arrangements for visitors and visiting parties, contact the Secretary (☎236 2794).

Beggars Wood Park: *Lobley Hill, Gateshead.* ☎460 0140
Introductory golf coaching courses are held on the nine-hole pitch and putt course. There is also a floodlit covered golf driving range.

Blyth Golf Club: *Plessey Rd, Newsham, Blyth.* ☎0670-356514
18-hole course, length 6533 yards, par 72. Membership £111 p.a. plus £90 joining fee. Open from 9am till dusk. Bar facilities, restaurant and shop, but no club hire.

Boldon Golf Club: *Dipe Lane, East Boldon.* ☎536 4182
6348 yards, 18 holes. Ladies tee off blue, men off white. Open any time, does not close. Restrictions on visitors. Bar and meals. Membership costs: men, full playing (Mon–Sun) £120, over 65 (5 days, Mon–Fri) £80; 18–21, from £65 to £150; junior, £65; women, full playing £140, plus other rates.

City of Newcastle Golf Club: *Three Mile Bridge, Gosforth, Newcastle.* ☎285 1775.
Par 72 course, 6508 yards. Green fees: weekdays, £9; weekends, £13. Visitors are welcome, but it's best to phone first. The professional and secretary is A.J. Matthews.

Gosforth Golf Club: *Broadway East, Gosforth, Newcastle.* ☎285 3495
Three miles north of Newcastle city centre off the A6127. 18 holes, 6030 yards. Green fees: weekdays, £8.50, £5 with a member; weekends/bank holidays, £12, £6 with a member. Eating facilities (order in advance). Visitors are welcome with reservation, arrange with Secretary.

Gosforth Park Golfing Complex: *High Gosforth Park, Gosforth.* ☎236 4480
6200 yards, par 71. Open from dawn till dusk. Membership (Oct–Oct): men £147 + £50 joining fee; women £78 + £50. Visitors welcome: Mon–Fri, £6; weekends, £7. No club hire available. 30 bay driving range; 9-hole pitch & putt. Bar and restaurant.

Heworth Golf Club: *Jingling Gate, Heworth, Gateshead.* ☎469 2137
Subscriptions: male member, £154; lady member, £106; male senior member, £70; female senior member, £60; country member, £106; junior member, £25 (10-14), £40 (14-16), £65 (16-18); social member, £1.50. Locker rental, £2. Joining fees: golf members, nil; social members, £3.

Hobson Golf Course: *Hobson, Burnopfield.* ☎0207-71605
This is a municipal golf course with all of its facilities open to the public. Annual subscription (adults): £106 (no joining fee). Daily green fees: weekdays, adults £4.50 & junior/OAPs £3.50; weekends/bank holidays, all players £6. Arrangements can be made for visiting parties. For further information contact the golf professional, Jack Ord (☎0207-71605).

Newcastle United Golf Club: *Ponteland Rd, Cowgate, Newcastle.* ☎286 4693
Two miles west of city centre, towards the airport. This is a private club nearing its centenary. The course is 18 holes par 72. Visitors are welcome. Green fees: weekdays

SPORT 151

Tynemouth Golf Club: *Spital Dene, Tynemouth.* ☎257 4578
6403 yards, part 70, standard scratch 71. Club hire and tuition for beginners by arrangement with the professional, John McKenna (☎258 0728). Visitors welcome if they are members of other clubs and have recognised handicaps. Fee for visitors: £10 midweek, £5 with member; £12 weekends, £6 with member.

Whitley Bay Golf Course: *Claremont Rd, Whitley Bay.*
☎252 0180
18-hole course, length 6617 yards. Standard scratch score 72. Green fees £10 daily, no visitors allowed at weekends, no club hire. Open from dawn till dusk.

GREYHOUNDS

Brough Park Stadium: *Fossway, Walker, Newcastle.* ☎265 8011
Greyhound racing every Tuesday, Thursday and Saturday evenings. Tuesday & Thursday, 7.30–10pm; Saturday, 7.20–10.10pm. Additional afternoon race meetings throughout the year which are relayed to betting shops throughout the country. Brough Park also has speedway racing every Sunday at 7pm from March until October and stock car racing every other Monday from April until November. The stadium has four public bars and a 130-seater glass-fronted à la carte restaurant, as well as snack bar facilities. Car parking for about 400 cars.

Pelaw Grange Greyhound Stadium: *Birtley, Co. Durham.* ☎410 2141
Track open all year round. Race nights: Mon, Thurs, Sat. Trial sessions: Sun (10.30am), Tues & Fri (1.30pm), and before racing (6.30pm). Admission £1, with reductions for OAPs and children. Track open 6.15pm; first race 7.30pm; last race usually 10.30pm; 13 races.

HORSE RACING

Gosforth Park: *Newcastle Racecourse, Gosforth, Newcastle.*
☎236 2020
Newcastle Racecourse is situated in over 800 acres of unspoilt parkland but is less than four miles from the city centre. The racecourse at High Gosforth Park stages top class flat and National Hunt racing on 19 days throughout the year. Admission charges: Club visitors, £12; junior Club visitors, £5; Tattersalls, £6; OAPs and disabled are admitted to the Club for £6 and to Tattersalls for £3; accompanied children under 16, free. Car and coach parking is free. The subscription for the Race Club is Lady or Gentleman, £60; Lady and Gentleman, £95; Junior (under 21), £25.

ICE SKATING & ICE HOCKEY

Durham Ice Rink: *Walkergate, Durham City.* ☎386 4065
The ice rink is open Monday–Thursday, 10–12am, 2–4.30pm & 6.30–9.30; Friday, 10–12am & 2–9.15pm disco; Saturday, 9–10am, Disney club; 10–12am, 2–4.30pm & 6.30–9pm; Sunday, 2–4.30pm & 6.30–9.30pm. There is usually an ice hockey match on Sunday evenings and therefore no evening ice skating session. Face off is at 6.30 p.m. The hockey season runs from September to April. Ice rink admission charges: adults, £1.20; children, £1.10; spectators, 40p; skate hire, 50p. Ice hockey admission charges: adults, £3.50; children, £2.

Whitley Bay Ice Rink: *Hillheads Rd, Whitley Bay.* ☎252 6240.
The ice rink provides a full ice hockey and ice skating training programme for all age groups. During the winter season ice hockey matches are staged on Sundays and occasionally on Saturday nights. The rink is the North East's largest indoor venue for pop concerts and major events. It is open seven days a week: mornings, 10am–12.30pm (except Sundays and Tuesdays); afternoons, 2–4.30pm (Tuesdays in school term, 3.30–6pm); evenings, 7–10pm (Sundays, 6.30–9.30pm). Admission charges: adults, £1.20; children, £1.10. There is also a ten pin bowling centre open daily from 10am until about midnight. Bowling charges: £1.10 per game, 10p shoe rental. Party bookings also taken.

MARTIAL ARTS & KEEP FIT

The Body Zone: *Carliol Sq, Newcastle.* ☎232 6882
Tucked away behind Worswick St bus station, The Body Zone is a health studio with two gymnasiums, an exercise and dance studio, and a licensed members bar. Facilities include freeweights, air dyne cycles, saunas, beauty treatments, aerobics classes and martial arts instruction.

Chojin Martial Arts: *10-12 Low Friar St, Newcastle.* ☎261 9859
Karate Introduction for beginner or Advanced for adults, teenagers, and children. The joining fee of £22.50 for seniors or £15 for juniors includes a free Karate suit and life membership. Class fees: senior, £2.50; junior, £2; reductions for the unemployed. The class is open seven days a week.

Dance City: *see* **Arts Centres.**

RIDING

Benridge Riding Centre: *Benridge Hagg, Morpeth, Northumberland.* ☎0670-518507
Situated in 26 acres of rural Northumberland, but only two miles from Morpeth and a mile from the A1 trunk road, the Benridge Riding Centre is open every day except Mondays. They have an all weather paddock which is floodlit in the autumn. Beginners to advance level riders welcome, children and adults, with classes or private lessons. No membership fees, details of lessons upon request.

Border Riding School: *The Stables, Wooler Road, Cornhill on Tweed, Northumberland.* ☎0890-2987
The Border school has been running for the past 15 years, seven days a week, all year round. As well as the normal day to day riding facilities, they can also offer a full breaking and schooling service. All ages are catered for with a selection of different sized horses and ponies. They also welcome the more experienced rider who may use the hobby as an ideal way of exploring the surrounding countryside.

Bowes Manor Stables: *North Side, Birtley, Chester-le-Street.* ☎410 9703
Open six days a week (closed on Mondays) from 9am till they finish. The cost of a hack in a group is £4 per hour, a private hack lesson or jumping lesson is £6. Hard hats are provided free of charge for the hour. The staff are very experienced and all the horses are well schooled and safe rides.

Kimmerston Riding Centre: *Milfield, Wooler, Northumberland.* ☎06686-283
Caters for all types, from absolute

beginners to very experienced riders. Open all year round. They say it is fantastic riding country and they can ensure that everyone who comes gets that extra little bit of excitement from horse riding.

Sinderhope Pony Trekking Centre: *High Sinderhope, Allenheads, Northumberland.* ☎043485-266
Sinderhope is situated in the heart of the once famous lead and silver mining country where traces of these workings can still be seen. Many of the treks follows paths once trodden by teams of pack ponies. The panoramic views are much more appreciated from horseback, with the Roman Wall country to the north. Previous riding experience isn't necessary to enjoy trekking as suitable ponies are selected for beginners. One hour and half-day treks available. Riding hats provided. Charges: £3 per hour.

Slate Hall Riding Centre: *Main St, North Sunderland, Seahouses, Northumberland.* ☎0665-720320
Open daily from 9.30pm. Evening rides by arrangement. The cost is £5 per hour. They offer riding holidays for both the novice and the advanced rider, and there are beaches on either side of the centre; a pony and trap is available for the non-rider.

SAILING

Derwent Reservoir Sailing Club: *Blanchland, Northumberland.* ☎043475-258
The reservoir, in a Pennine valley on the borders of Northumberland and Durham, is one of the largest manmade lakes in Britain, three and a half miles long. Activities here include fishing, birdwatching and sailing. The sailing club was formed in 1967 and has its clubhouse and 400 dinghy berths on the north shore. Membership charges: entry fee, £25; ordinary member, £26; family, £42; junior, £13; student, outport, £15; boat/sailboard fee, £17.

Royal Northumbrian Yacht Club: *South Harbour, Blyth.* ☎0670-353636
Private club. Membership: £57 p.a; age 18-25, £29; family, £69; husband, wife and (age 7-18) cadet, £77.50. Visitors have to be signed in. Membership entitles you to use the bar facilities, showers and galley (which serves meals). Private boat owners look to the club for crews for racing or pleasure trips. Membership enquiries: Ian & Margaret McKenzie, ☎252 5207.

South Shields Sailing Club: *43 Lane Rd, South Shields.* ☎456 1506
The club has organised racing in the harbour and at sea (weather permitting), with nine classes of boats. Subscriptions for a full year: full member (21 and over), £39; youth member (18-20), £29; family member, £10; cadet member (14-17), £10. Formed in 1957, the club puts on a varied social programme, including barbecues, discos, quiz nights, ceilidhs and social evenings.

Tynemouth Sailing Club: *Priors Haven, Tynemouth.* ☎257 2617
A members-only club which takes the teaching of its beginners and coaching of intermediate sailors very seriously. Friday night training has proved very successful. The club is well equipped with a comfortable lounge bar, a wet bar, kitchen and changing rooms.

SKIING

Ski Slope Centre: *Cottingwood*

Lane, Morpeth, Northumberland.
☎0670-517360.
Dry ski slope owned by Northumberland Education Committee mainly used by school parties from north of Tyne Lea, but the public can also use the slope. Pre-booked block bookings are needed, with a minimum of 10 people. For booking and cost information, contact County Hall, Morpeth ☎0670-514343 x 3644). The cost includes boots, skis and ski poles plus instruction. They ask parties to arrive 30 minutes before time stated to allow for kitting up. Gloves are essential!

SNOOKER & POOL

Central Snooker Club: *Centre House, New Bridge St, Newcastle.* ☎261 6559
Open 10am–11.30pm. £1.95/hr before 5pm, £2.31/hr later. Membership £5 p.a. 11 tables. Licensed bar.

The Hustler: *Northumberland St, Newcastle.* ☎232 9137
Private club open 11am–11pm. Membership £6 p.a. (£2.50 to renew), students £2.50. 20p to 50p per game depending upon quality of table. Tables: 15 pool, 5 snooker. Two licensed bars, bar meals at lunchtimes.

Mr G's Snooker Club: *Groat House, Groat Mkt, Newcastle.* ☎261 2185
Open 11am–11pm; Sundays from 7pm. Free membership. Tables: 3 snooker, 4 pool. Snooker £1 per half hour, pool 30p per game. Licensed bar, with bar meals at lunchtimes.

On Cue Snooker Club: *Old Co-op Buildings, North St, Jarrow.*
☎489 2250
Open 11am–11pm. Membership £2 p.a, children £1 p.a, life membership £10. £1.25/hr during day, £1.75/hr evenings. Visitors (20p) welcome if signed in. Licensed bar, bar snacks.

Riley Snooker Club: *High Bridge, Newcastle.* ☎232 0104.
Open 11am–11pm, seven days a week. Membership £6 p.a. Age limit 18. Snooker, £2.28/hr. No pool. 14 snooker tables. £1 guest fee. Snacks available.

Supasnooker: *Old Hibernian Club, Potts St, Byker,* ☎265 9918 & *Paradise Methodist Church, Atkinson Rd, Benwell, Newcastle,* ☎272 3241
Open 11am–11pm. £1.50/hr before 6pm, £1.98/hr later. Membership £5 p.a. Licensed bar, bar snacks. Visitors (£1) welcome if signed in. Byker has 18 tables plus a gym; Benwell has 17 snooker tables and one pool table.

Whitley Lodge Snooker Club: *Claremont Cres, Whitley Bay.* ☎251 1997
Membership £2 per month. £2/hr for a game. Open: summer, 2–11.30pm; winter, 11am–11pm. Non-members sign in for £1. Tables: 14 snooker, 1 pool. Licensed bar.

SPEEDWAY

Brough Park Stadium: *Fossway, Walker, Newcastle.* ☎265 8011
Speedway racing every Sunday at 7pm from March until September and stock car racing every other Monday from April until November. Admission: adults £4, children £1.50. Teams of motorbike riders race in a league, and the home team is Newcastle Diamonds. You can watch from the terraces or under cover from one of the four bars or from the 130-seater glass-fronted à

la carte restaurant. Car parking for about 400 cars.

SQUASH & TENNIS

Gateshead Squash & Fitness Club: *Joicey Rd, Low Fell.* ☎487 1981
Membership £60, £30 off peak. Costs £2 for 40 mins for members before 5pm, £2.80 later; or £1.50 for 30 mins before 5pm, £1.80 later. Guest fee £1. Open: 9.30am–11pm. Bar and bar meals.

Jesmond Dene Real Tennis Club: *Matthew Bank, Jesmond Dene, Newcastle.* ☎281 6854
Real tennis is now making a comeback. It's the game as played by Henry VIII, a cross between tennis and squash, and the Jesmond Dene club is one of only 20 in the country. Memberships is £30 p.a. for adults, students £20, juniors £10. Court hire, £6/hr; racket hire, £1. The court is indoors, and open from 9am to 11pm daily. The professional is Robert Moyle, and non-members can contact him to arrange a game.

Northumberland Lawn Tennis & Squash Rackets Club: *North Jesmond Ave, Jesmond, Newcastle.* ☎281 5858
The courts comprise: six grass, three floodlit, nine all-weather tarmac, six synthetic grass, five squash, plus one indoors for tennis or badminton. The club is open from 9am to 10.30pm every day, 364 days a year; the bar is open lunchtimes and evenings during the week and on Sundays, and from midday till 10.30pm on Saturdays. Joining fee £25 or £10 for under-25s; various annual subscription rates depending upon age and usage, including senior sport £120, student or under-18 sport £50, unemployed £60 (paid quarterly), social £20 or family £250. New members are introduced to other members and can become involved in league and informal play right-away.

SWIMMING

The City Pool: *Northumberland Rd, Newcastle.* ☎232 1981
Three swimming pools, a sports injury clinic, fitness room, sauna, sunbeds and the city's only genuine Turkish bath. The large 25m pool is used for programmed fitness swimming and major events. Swimming lessons for adults (beginners and improvers) run for most of the year, with special private sessions for parents and toddlers, women and OAPs, and on Tuesday lunchtimes they have 'Splashdance' Keep Fit sessions for women. Newcastle Amateur Swimming Club also organises training at various levels, from the Shrimps Squad for children, to water polo and synchronised swimming. Pool open: Mon, 12am–7.30pm; Tues–Thurs, 8.30am–7.30pm; Fri, 8.30am–6.30pm; Sat, 8.30am–4.30pm; last admissions half an hour before closing.

Jesmond Swimming Baths: *St Georges Tce, Jesmond, Newcastle.* ☎281 2482.
Open: Mon, 12am–5.30pm & adults only 5.30–8.30pm; Tues, 12am–7.30pm; Wed, 12am–7pm; Thurs, 12am–1pm, 2.30–6.30pm & (women's aqua-aerobics) 7.30–8.30pm; Fri, 12am–7.30pm; Sat, 8.30–10am & 1–4pm; Sun, 1.30–3.30pm; last admission is half an hour before closing, and the opening hours are extended during school holidays; closed on bank holidays. Jesmond Pool also has a solarium and swim shop, and puts on swimming classes for juniors, adults and parents & tots; beginners' lessons are on Wednesday evenings.

Tynemouth Indoor Pool: *North Shields, Tynemouth.* ☎257 8137
Tynemouth organises swimming lessons: children, Mon–Fri, 4.30–5.30pm; adults, Wed, 7.30–9.30pm. Also diving lessons, 7.30–9.30pm on Wednesdays for both children and adults. Mother and toddler group on Thursday. Lesson prices: adult, £13; junior, £8.55; under-5s, £4.25. Swimming prices: adult, 85p; junior, 30p; under-5s, 20p. Spectator prices: adult, 35p; junior, 15p; under-5s free.

Whitley Bay Leisure Pool: *Whitley Bay.* ☎253 1955
This is fun for all the family with an Aquarena Water Slide, large free-shaped leisure pool, shallow water beach, wave machine, diving and teaching pools. Prices for swimming range from 95p for adults to 20p for under-5s.

WATER SPORTS

Newton-by-the-Sea Windsurfing Centre: *Low Newton Farm, Newton-by-the-Sea, Alnwick.* ☎0665-76452
Hire available to the public during Whit and summer school holidays at £3 per hour or £10 per day. Tuition also available.

Northumbrian Seasports: *Kahana Park, Beadnell Bay, Northumberland,* ☎0665-721213 & *Windygale Outdoor Sports Centre,* ☎0668-3289
Run in conjunction with Windygale: tuition approx. £20 for canoeing or windsurfing, including all equipment and log book. Takes place at Beadnell Bay, rear caravan park.

Northumbrian Windsurfing Centre: *7-9 City Rd, Newcastle.* ☎232 5556
Windsurfing at Wansbeck Boat-sailing School, Queen Elizabeth Park, Ashington. Five-hour course costs £25. Hire for those already skilled costs £15 per day or £4 per hour.

Reivers of Tarset: *Leaplish Waterside Park, Kielder Water.* ☎0660-50203
Offer instruction in windsurfing, canoeing, motorboats and sailboats (all for hire). Windsurfer hire £5–£13, 2½hr course £16 inc. equipment. Canoeing instruction £10/hr. Group rates (for 12 people): 2 out of 3 activities, £8 per head for 2½hrs, £16 per day. Canadian canoes with camping gear also available: book in advance. Open all week, 10.30–6pm.

Roker Watersports Centre: *Marine Walk, Roker, Sunderland.* ☎565 6662
Windsurfing: £7.50 per half day, £10 per full day (or £2.50 & £10 if you come from Sunderland). Kayaks: £2.50 per half day, £5 per full day (Sunderland people, £1 & £2). Special rates for UB40 holders. Open in summer till dusk.

South Durham Windsurfing: *Bishopton Lake, Stoney Flatts, nr Stockton.* ☎0740-31057/30518
Sailing venue in open, windy countryside, minutes from the A1(M), with amenity building, shop, licensed bar; overnight accommodation available in the gatehouse. Open 10am–9pm. Board hire: £6 for first hour then £2/hr, inc. wet suit. Tuition charges: £6/hr for one person; £4/hr for two; £3/hr for three; £2/hr over four. Instruction (inc. all equipment hire): RYA Level 1 (beginners course) £30, Saturdays 10am–5pm; Introductory Beginners Course (min. 2 persons) £12 (2 hours).

SPORTS CENTRES

Eldon Square Recreation Centre: *entrance Nelson St, Newcastle.* ☎232 5999
Opened in 1976, the Centre is used by 16,000 people a week. Badminton and five-a-side are played in the Main Hall, which also accommodates conferences, shows, and basketball and snooker matches. The eight-rink international bowling green is used for league and competition play from April to September, as well as casual bowls for non-members; from October to March the area converts to a centre for exhibitions and functions or a children's soft play and activity area. There are also six squash courts, a solarium/sauna, bars and a restaurant. Other activities include snooker, table tennis, aerobics, fitness training and martial arts. There are always new things happening at Eldon Square: call in at the reception for the latest information. Open from 9am: Mon–Fri & Sun till 10.30pm, Sat till 6pm.

Gateshead International Stadium: *Neilson Rd, Gateshead.* ☎478 1687
Events include international athletics meetings, cross country meetings, football and rugby matches, and badminton, gymnastics and carpet bowls tournaments. In the winter the stadium is the home ground of Gateshead Football Club; in the summer Gateshead International Senators play American football in the Budweiser League (Sundays, kick-off 3pm). The stadium has been voted the top British venue for radio-controlled cars. As well as spectator sports, the stadium offers a packed activity programme including athletics, badminton, basketballl, boxing, fencing, five-a-side, football, golf, gymnastics, hockey, keep fit, martial arts, orienteering, table tennis, tennis, volleyball, weightlifting. The lunchtime road race series gives you the opportunity to compete with beginners and international athletes: the handicapping system gives everyone a chance. Open from 9am: Mon–Fri till 10pm, Sat & Sun till 9pm.

Gateshead Leisure Centre: *Alexandra Rd, Gateshead.* ☎477 3975
Events include five-a-side, basketball (Gateshead Vikings and Tyne Tees Ladies), netball (international matches), volleyball, karate, dog shows, fish shows, flower shows, Mr & Mrs England (body building), darts (Autumn Gold Masters Finals), concerts and pantomimes. Facilities: aerobics, badminton, ballroom dancing, basketball, cricket, dancing, five-a-side, gymnastics, keep fit, martial arts, netball, sauna, soft play, solarium, squash, swimming, table tennis, tennis, trampolining, Turkish baths, yoga. Open: Mon–Sun, 9am–10pm.

Ashington Leisure Centre: *Institute Rd, Ashington.* ☎0670-813254
Facilities: airbed, badminton, boxing, canoeing, five-a-side, gymnastics, indoor bowls, indoor cricket, indoor hockey, karate, keep fit, sauna, snooker, soft play, solarium, squash, suncradle, swimming, table tennis, trampolining, weight-training. Open: Mon, Tues, Wed, Fri, 10am–10.30pm; Thurs, 12am–10.30pm; Sat, Sun, 9am–10.30pm.

Blyth Sports Centre: *Bolam Park, Blyth.* ☎0670-352943
Facilities: aerobics, badminton, ballroom dancing, bar, bowls, five-a-side, gymnastics, jacuzzi, martial arts, netball, nursery, pop-mobility, roller-skating, sauna, soft play, solarium, squash, swimming, table tennis, tennis. Open: Mon–Sun, 9am–11pm.

Castle Ward Sports Centre: *Callerton Lane, Ponteland, Newcastle.* ☎0661-25441
Facilities: aerobics, archery, badminton, bar, basketball, chess, creche, cricket, darts, disabled, fitness room, five-a-side, football, indoor bowls, jacuzzi, netball, restaurant, rugby, running track, sauna, solarium, squash, table tennis, tennis, trim track, volleyball, yoga. Open: Mon–Sun, 9am–11pm.

Concordia Sports Centre: *Forum Way, Town Centre, Cramlington.* ☎0670-717423
Facilities: badminton, bar, basketball, cafeteria, climbing wall, creche, disabled, five-a-side, football, gymnastics, indoor bowls, judo, karate, netball, pop mobility, sauna, snooker, softplay (July–August), solarium, squash, sunbeds, swimming, table tennis, trampolining, volleyball, weightlifting, yoga. Open: Mon–Sun, 9am–11pm.

Cowgate Leisure Centre: *Harehills Ave, Kenton, Newcastle.* ☎286 9521
Facilities: American football, badminton, darts, five & seven-a-side, gymnastics, keep fit, martial arts, netball, pool, softplay, table tennis, trampolining, volleyball, weight-training. Open from 9am: Mon–Fri till 9.30pm, Sat & Sun till 4.30pm.

Dunston Activity Centre: *Ellison Rd, Dunston, Gateshead.* ☎460 5000
Activities include aerobics, badminton, basketball, body conditioning, five-a-side, gymnastics, keep fit, tennis, trampolining, volleyball, weight-training, yoga and machine knitting. Several clubs use the centre for karate, judo, netball, badminton, carpet bowls, weight watching and photography. Facilities include a library, coffee shop, bar, fitness room and creche. Open from 9am: Mon–Fri till 10pm, Sat till 4pm, Sun till 1pm.

Elswick Park Leisure Centre: *Elswick Rd, Newcastle.* ☎273 7801
Facilities: aerobics, bowling, canoeing, five-a-side, keep fit, life saving, swimming, table tennis. Open: Mon–Sun, 9am–9pm (closed weekday mornings for schools).

Killingworth Sports Centre: *Citadel East, Killingworth, Newcastle.* ☎268 3535
Facilities: archery, badminton, bar, canoeing, cricket, five-a-side, gymnastics, hockey, judo, netball, pop mobility, roller skating, soft play, squash, sunbeds, swimming (lessons and life saving), subaqua, tennis, trampolining, volleyball, weightlifting. Open from 9am: Mon–Fri till 10.30pm, Sat & Sun till 4.30pm.

Lightfoot Centre: *Wharrier St, Walker, Newcastle.* ☎265 5597
Indoor facilities: two court main sports hall, weight training room, soft play, squash courts, cafe, bar, function suite, combat room, conference facilities and creche. Outdoor facilities (all floodlit): synthetic track and full athletics facility, synthetic turf pitches and grass soccer pitch. Activities: five & six-a-side football, athletics (Heaton Harriers), badminton, gymnastics, judo, trampolining, snooker, basketball, volleyball, netball, table tennis and pool. Open from 9am: Mon–Fri till 10.30pm, Sat & Sun till 4.30pm.

Newburn Leisure Centre: *Grange Rd, Newburn, Newcastle.* ☎264 0014
Facilities: badminton, basketball, carpet bowls, five & seven-a-side football, hockey (indoor & outdoor), indoor cricket & tennis, netball, river activities, snooker, soccer, softplay, table tennis, volleyball, weight-training. Open from 9am: Mon–Fri till 10pm, Sat & till 5pm.

Park View Sports Centre: *Annfield Rd, North Kenton, Newcastle.*
☎271 5143
Facilities: archery, badminton, baseball, basketball, café, creche, five-a-side, indoor bowls, judo, lacrosse, netball, quick cricket, tennis, trampolining, volleyball, weight-training. Open from 9am: Mon–Sat till 9pm, Sat & Sun till 5.30pm.

Rye Hill Sports Centre: *Newcastle College, Maple Tce, Newcastle.*
☎273 8675
Facilities: aerobics, aikido, badminton, basketball, cricket, five-a-side, gymnastics, judo, kali (Filipino martial art), karate, keep fit, netball, power jog, table tennis, tae kwondo, Thai boxing, trampolining, weight-training. Open from 9am: Mon–Fri till 10pm, Sun till 5pm; summer, Mon–Fri 2–10pm only; Sat, closed.

Scotswood Sports & Social Centre: *Denton Rd, Newcastle.*
☎274 3716
Facilities: badminton, basketball, cricket, disco, football, gymnastics, judo, keep fit, netball, pool, roller disco, soft play, table tennis, tennis, trampolining. Open from 8am: Mon–Fri & Sun till 10pm, Sat till 6pm.

Temple Park Leisure Centre: *John Reid Rd, South Shields.* ☎456 9119
Facilities: aerotone, air-play park, bar and cafeteria, gymnastics hall, multi-gym, sauna, softplay, solarium, synthetic football pitch, table tennis, trampolining, weightlifting. Open: Mon & Fri, 12.30–8pm; Tues, Wed & Thurs, 1.30–8pm; Sat & Sun, 10am–5pm.

Wallsend Sports Centre: *Rheydt Ave, Bigges Main, Wallsend.*
☎262 9431
Facilities: athletics, badminton, bar, bowls, cafeteria, cricket, dancing, darts, five-a-side, football, golf, gymnastics, inflatable castle, judo, netball, rugby, shooting, squash, table tennis, tennis, trampolining, tukido, volleyball, weightlifting, whippets. Open from 9am: Mon–Fri till 10pm, Sat & Sun till 5pm.

Washington Golf & Squash Centre: *George Washington Hotel, Stone Cellar Rd, District 12, Washington.*
☎417 2626
Facilities: club-golf, computerised bike, driving range, golf, jacuzzi, leisure club, multi gym, sauna, snooker, solarium, squash, swimming. Open: snooker & leisure club, 9am–11pm; golf shop, 7.30am–8pm.

Other large sports centres in the North-East: **Consett Sports Centre** (☎0207-505011); **Crowtree Leisure Centre,** Sunderland (☎514 2511); **Easington District Leisure Centre,** Peterlee (☎586 5261); the **Louisa Sports Centre,** Stanley (☎0207-230311); and **Spectrum Leisure Complex,** Crook (☎0388-747000).

If you have any comments about this guide, or material for possible inclusion in the next edition, write to Richard Falkner at Bloodaxe Books (Projects) Ltd, P.O. Box 1SN, Newcastle upon Tyne NE99 1SN.